EFFECTIVE RADIO SPEAKING

EFFECTIVE
RADIO SPEAKING

BY

William G. Hoffman

Professor of English and Public Speaking
College of Business Administration, Boston University

AND

Ralph L. Rogers

Radio Writer-Producer;
Director of Radio Courses at Boston University;
Author of "Do's and Dont's
of Radio Writing"

First Edition
Second Impression

McGRAW-HILL BOOK COMPANY, INC.

NEW YORK AND LONDON

1944

PREFACE

Radio audiences of twenty years ago may have had the right idea. They wouldn't tolerate speeches on the air. They wanted songs, music, laughs—entertainment without education or uplift. They told station directors what they thought of those sly camouflages by which harmless little two- or three-minute speeches were sneaked over on an innocent and unsuspecting public. Speakers had their place and it was the platform. It was an outrage to have them butt in on this new radio and invade the citizen's privacy with "the windy satisfactions of their tongues."

Times have changed. Announcers today can introduce speakers as if they are really wanted and actually welcome. Big names and special topics have their drawing power. But the public has not changed so much as the times. It is still allergic to speakers. It does not protest so vigorously as in the early days of radio because it has more stations to find refuge in. Speakers are still mostly pleasing themselves instead of audiences.

Yet there are speakers who do hold attention. They have life, color, and a trained skill in making their subjects interesting to listeners. They have something to say and know how to say it. They are radio personalities who always have an audience.

A few speakers have an instinct that guides them to effective contact with listeners, but the great majority get nowhere in spite of intelligence and education because they

v

are not properly aware of the fundamental psychology involved in the successful writing and reading of script for radio. Many a good platform speaker is a failure behind the microphone and, on the other hand, some very effective radio performers are dull on the platform.

The fact is that the script, which, on first thought, would seem to make everything easier, is the stumbling block that bars at least 90 per cent of speakers from satisfactory achievement on the air. If they are lucky enough to compose good scripts, they are still very liable to make a mess of the reading.

You see what we're getting at. If you have enough of the writer and the actor in you, don't bother to read this book. But if you want some systematic discussion of what makes a good radio talk good, and some advice that may give your talk the spark you are vaguely looking for, we hope you will find them here. It is for you that this book is written.

WILLIAM G. HOFFMAN,

RALPH L. ROGERS.

BOSTON UNIVERSITY,
   May, 1944.

ACKNOWLEDGMENTS

We are indebted to many persons and publishing houses for the use of speeches and other illustrative material in this book. For permission to quote freely from significant recent articles and speeches we wish to make special acknowledgment to the following publications:

Talks, a quarterly digest of addresses given over the Columbia network and published by the Columbia Broadcasting System, Inc., 485 Madison Avenue, New York City. From *Talks* we have reprinted in part or in full addresses by Wendell Willkie, Herbert Hoover, Sir William Beveridge, James Lawrence Fly, Edward R. Murrow, Eric Sevareid, Harry S. Gradle, and Walton E. Cole.

Vital Speeches, published twice a month by the City News Publishing Company, New York City. From *Vital Speeches* we have reprinted a speech by Dr. D. F. Fleming.

Town Meeting, the bulletin of *America's Town Meeting of the Air*, published by American Education Press, Inc., Columbus, Ohio. From *Town Meeting* we have reprinted talks by Sol Lewis, Lewis Browne, and David Seabury.

The University of Chicago Round Table. We have reprinted in full, from pamphlet number 282, "The Economic System—Today and Tomorrow," a radio discussion by William Benton, Eric Johnston, and Harold J. Laski.

The Nation, published by The Nation Associates, Inc., 55 Fifth Avenue, New York City. From *The Nation* we have reprinted Jonathan Daniel's "The Hour of Elation."

vii

CONTENTS

→≫→≫≪←≪←

CONTENTS

EFFECTIVE RADIO SPEAKING

CHAPTER I

What Is Radio Personality?

"Yes," concluded the director, "it's no wonder everybody has a hankering to go on the air. You see, the glamour boys and girls don't have it all their own way here. Those good looks and bright eyes, that captivating smile, don't mean a thing on the radio. The mousy little chap with the bald head, big ears, and bleary eyes may put it over better than the big boy of the platform or the stage.

"And I'm glad of it. The homely folks and the frustrated tenth of the population are getting their innings now."

"Just a minute!" we protested, as he got up to lead us out. "Those giraffes or rabbits or monkeys have still got to have something. What is it?"

"You forgot to mention donkeys," retorted the too friendly old-timer, poking us in the ribs. "They are stubborn, make silly noises, and refuse to move when you give them a hint. Of course they've got to have something, but it isn't the same thing for everyone. Look over the crowd that's made good and puzzle it out for yourselves. I'll give you all the time you want on that $64 question." And he waved us off as he went to his next program.

We were disappointed that he didn't commit himself to something about radio personality or give us a formula for getting attention and holding it. Still, generalities and definitions are mostly weasel words, and there is always the drudgery of trying to do what you think they mean.

The director was wise, though. Something can be learned by thoughtful listening. Even if the variety of styles and voices may seem at first only bewildering, a little study may show that they have a few vital elements in common. There may be a pattern or a system or just an informal method that all good speakers observe consciously or unconsciously.

Suppose we tune in on a local station. It would be a "commercial." You never can escape that for long. Has any advertising man ever written one that you want to listen to? And yet they say that advertising on the radio is enormously profitable. Must be the program. But it's got to have a name, a company label, to identify it—and that name is repeated so often that it sinks in. H'mm, repetition. Could that be a guiding principle?

On the other hand, if we don't like commercials this rubbing it in may only drive us mad. The advertiser knows this, of course, and tries to curry favor by more or less ingenious tricks. Some days he creeps up on us; at other times he slugs us without apology. Then he trots out his toys to amuse us—fog horns, whistles, bells, talking dogs, parrots, cows. He rinsowhites and moderndesigns. He coos with lullabies or mixes drinks. When you hope he's gone for the night, he suddenly pops up like a jack-in-a-box, elbows the comedian to one side, and goes whimsical about his product.

He feels guilty. He knows we hate to take the medicine, but it's good for us and he tries in a variety of ways to make it less distressing.

Variety! Is this an important element of persuasion? Coupled with repetition it sounds contradictory, not to say crippling. We'll have to consider this paradox more care-fully. The advertisers can really teach us a great deal about effective expression, but just now we're on the trail of some-thing else.

It is among the news commentators, the politicians, the travelers, the teachers, preachers, and occasional speakers with somewhat humdrum subjects that we are most likely to discover the clues to good radio talk. And to make the search as brief and practical as possible we had better confine ourselves, for the time being, to those well-known speakers you have all heard. You can compare your own impressions with ours and use your own experi-ence and observation as a more dependable aid.

Perhaps it is natural to think first of the men with voices—men like Edwin C. Hill, Lowell Thomas, John B. Kennedy, and Frazier Hunt. It is discouraging, too, for most of us think we have to get along with run-of-the-mill voices. Of course that's not so. A large part of this book is based on the premise that all normally healthy voices can be made agreeable and interesting.

But listen to Mr. Hill. He has the sonorous, chanting resonance of the orator. He sounds as though he had spent much of his youth rehearsing "Friends, Romans, country-men, lend me your ears," or

> Roll on, thou deep and dark blue ocean, roll!
> Ten thousand fleets sweep over thee in vain.

As a matter of fact, you ought to practice those and similar exercises we wish to expose you to, because by intoning such passages with a little dramatic exaggeration you will get your voice up out of your throat (the "mud," radiomen call it) and out on your lips. You can then project it with some of the winging, soaring quality that is Mr. Hill's trade-mark.

On second thought, is it chiefly Mr. Hill's voice that accounts for his success? Of course not. Indeed, some critics would even say that his voice is really inappropriate for radio because it lacks the personal, intimate, informal, chatty quality that should go with talk to the family at suppertime. That would be a superficial comment, however. Put a question mark here while we hurry along.

Lowell Thomas's voice has a similar rich vibrancy of tone, but it is more composed in rate. It is not so definitely dramatic.

John B. Kennedy might be a retired English actor who has decided that radio is just the spot to put that full-bodied, authoritative, and somewhat stabbing diction back to work. Add a touch of wayward, sardonic humor and you have a kind of jaunty assurance that has the authority of success.

Frazier Hunt has a mellow voice, almost lush, the very thing for the warm emotional tone he often uses. He dares to be a little more sentimental than the others and can speak tenderly of old pals and of afflicted and forgotten men.

Before you give up let's listen in to some of the voices with less obvious oomph. We hope Raymond Gram Swing won't be embarrassed if we start with him. If you were a foreigner and didn't understand English, what impression would you get from his tones? Wouldn't they seem rather thin, breathless, and characterized by a curious, monotonous rhythm? And yet, Mr. Swing is at the very top of his profession and regarded by many thoughtful listeners as the best commentator on the air. His voice is not unpleasant but would scarcely rate high on a teacher's objective chart. But you will admit that it commands respect and good will the moment it is heard. It is indeed a "trade-marked" voice, peculiar and distinctive, suggesting courtesy, character, and sensitive intelligence.

What about Elmer Davis? The speech teacher would try to do things to him, but his dry, slightly nasal and perfunctory quality gets by very well. We like him just because he has no frills. He sounds like a lot of us and tells a plain, unvarnished tale with a direct conciseness and lack of personal flourish that give him the common touch in the affection of millions.

William L. Shirer is another favorite speaker whose voice is that of the amateur rather than that of the professional. It is somewhat negative, lacking in attack and force, but his modest, subdued, and questioning inflections are pleasantly informal and sympathetic. Nice chap, we think. Hasn't got a swelled head over his best seller and his fame as a war correspondent. Sounds rather shy for a pushing reporter.

What about the women in radio? There are plenty of good actresses but not many well-known speakers or writers. Dorothy Thompson is, of course, outstanding because she is almost alone in her forthrightness, indignation, and eloquence. The besetting weakness of most women is their tame and colorless writing and their lack of personal dash.

Perhaps we have heard enough by this time to examine our scattered impressions for those recurring factors of personality. These will indicate important steps in our course of study.

Every speaker, naturally, desires good voice, and he ought to improve, as well as he can, what nature gave him. The point we tried to make in our little radio review, however, is that no one need be depressed if he has only a mediocre voice, and that other matters may be more fundamental in the making of a radio personality.

First, you may ask, what is personality? Not an easy question. You may look it up in the dictionary and discover how meaningless definitions can be. Among them, however, is "magnetic personal quality." *Magnetic* is the word that gives us pause. It means having something that draws or attracts. For radio it is not personal appearance. It can only be voice or something reflected by voice. But good voice alone will not hold us, and we have observed that so-so voices will do to convey other elements that are constant factors of interest.

Some of these other elements are easy to identify. What is the first thing we want from the commentators? Not abundantly magnetic voice, but news. "Well," you may reply, "that's too bad. That's one thing I'm not likely to have."

But don't be so sure. You are thinking of war news, of newspaper headlines. Your wise commentator knows that by the time you get around to him his news may be as stale as yesterday's newspaper. He has another line of approach. "You've heard the news," he says, in effect. "What do you make of it? It seems to me. . . . There are several possibilities here. . . . The Allies could do this. . . . The Axis could do that . . . ."

This is news, too, of another sort, usually called interpretation or analysis, and sometimes so ingenious that we mutter, "I wish he hadn't told all that; he's tipping Hitler off to some pretty smart stuff." At other times the commentator will single out bits that he hopes his rivals have overlooked. Lowell Thomas often signs off with a humorous triviality or a unique believe-it-or-not incident of no significance. It appeals to the "escape" motive of entertainment.

Every talk you may give on the radio is likely to contain news, information, something your audience did not know before. But that is not enough. Your news must be wanted, and your perpetual problem is to make it wanted. You can do that by developing what the writers of business letters call the "you-attitude." Do you see that family sitting around the radio? Do you know their desires, motives, aspirations? Are you a pretty fair salesman, a person who knows a good deal about his "prospects," as well as about his product? We are now only listing things, but you can be sure that interesting news may be found in any subject if the speaker is trained in the you-attitude.

Looking back at the speakers we have considered, we may discover another common element in good talk, the element of drama. *Drama* is a Greek word meaning action. Every drama is composed of movement, obstacles, conflict, and suspense. The skilled speaker finds drama not only in the war but in every topic. He finds its hidden root of universal interest and plans his attack against the challenge and obstacles of difference. He uses the strategy of the dramatist in coaxing initial attention, in providing situations, comparisons, and contrast, in building up approval for his theme, in sustaining attention by variety and surprise, and in leaving his audience intellectually and emotionally stirred. He has learned to convert routine, commonplace narration or exposition into living, pulsing drama.

You will agree, we think, that self-reliance is another characteristic of good speakers. You feel that they are not merely readers of books and quoters of other men's opinions. They have wrestled with ideas and trusted their own experience and instincts.

Self-reliance suggests vitality, the force that projects ideas with energy and enterprise. There is nothing languid, anemic, or flat about the effective personality.

And the personality should naturally have the personal touch. Sounds rather vague. Maybe it's just style—and don't ask us to be any clearer right now. For the moment, we give you two classic remarks to ponder. "The style is the man himself," said Buffon. Voltaire is more specific. "Nearly always," he declares, "the things a writer says are less striking than the way he puts them; for men in general have much the same ideas about the matters that form the stock in trade of all. It is the expression, the style, that makes all the difference."

We close this chapter with the most obvious element of radio personality: the ability to read a script so that it sounds like interested, animated, spontaneous talk. The broadcast is a failure if this element is missing. To some, it is a gift; so easy that it is not worth mentioning. To most, however, it is an art acquired only by considerable study and practice.

Here is a chart made up of topics and questions about personality as it is revealed by radio. If it includes items not mentioned before in this preliminary glance, be patient. Details will follow. You might call this a

RADIO REFLECTOR

It will remind you what to pack as equipment when you get ready for your turn in the studio. Rehearse before members of your family and ask them to check this list.

1. Voice.
    Is your tone cheerful, bright, alert?
    Is your tone nasal, or throaty, or muffled?
    Do you read at a comfortable, moderate rate of speed, about 140 words a minute?
    Do you avoid monotony by the use of pause and varied modulation?
    Do you sound as though you were talking with your audience and not just reading a paper?

2. Diction.

Do you speak clearly and without effort?

Do your speech habits reflect a background of education?

Do you leave out letters and syllables, say *lib'ry* for *library*, *recunize* for *recognize*, *reelly* for *re-al-ly*, *reg'lar* for *regular*?

Do you say *doody* for *duty* (dyuty), *noos* for *news*, *ackerate* for *accurate*, *manuhfacture* for *manyufacture*?

Do you say *jis'* for *just*, *gonna* for *going to*?

Have you a good dictionary?

Are you sure you are pronouncing all the words of your script correctly?

Do you open your mouth well in speaking?

Do you prolong your vowels and give your consonants distinctly and neatly?

3. News.

Does your script play up the most interesting item in your subject?

Have you related it to some current matter of importance?

Have you asked your audience to do anything about it?

4. You-attitude.

Have you considered why anyone should listen to you talk on this subject?

Have you appealed to any special motive in your listeners— making or saving money, fear of loss or injury to themselves or their families, success, loyalty, generosity, etc.?

Have you written the script with a special group, or type of person, in mind?

Is your language colloquial rather than literary?

Do you say *you* more frequently than *I*?

5. Self-reliance.

Does the script sound like you?

Does it sound as if you were echoing books and pamphlets too much?

Have you made the ideas a part of your own fundamental thinking?

Do you illustrate them by reference to your own experience?

Do you try to apply them to the experience of your listeners?

Are you confident without being dogmatic—too sure in regard to disputed matters?

6. Vitality.

Do you reflect a natural enthusiasm?

Do you stress underscored words and phrases enough to show their significance?

Is your force that of interested, friendly talk, or does it sound too much like oratory?

Do you pound along monotonously?

7. Drama (Showmanship).

Does your first sentence deliberately strike at the attention of your audience?

Is it natural and honest, yet intriguing?

Is there challenge, argument, surprise in your talk?

Have you posed a problem and presented a solution?

Have you selected the right purpose for your talk? Are you just informing, or are you trying to win belief or to get your audience to take some action?

Have you enough situations, illustrations, and anecdotes to make your points clear, enjoyable, emphatic?

Have you "given away" the theme of your talk in your opening paragraph, or have you maintained curiosity and suspense to the end?

If your talk is educational, is it also entertaining and inspiring?

Would an interview, a dialogue, serve your purpose better?

8. Style.

Did you make a plan or outline before writing the manuscript?

Is there progress and climax in the arrangement of your material?

Are your sentences short? Are they varied in length and form?

Have you enough connectives and transitional phrases?

Are your words specific—picture words?

Did you avoid trite expressions, overworked fancy phrases?
Are you sincere and direct?
Is there too much explanation?
Have you reduced generalities to "for instances"?
Have you tried to get a little humor out of your subject?
Is your style personal and chatty, or is it impersonal and heavy?

CHAPTER II
They Call It Showmanship

What they mean by it, these radio managers don't explain very clearly. In fact, they're often cloudy and mystic. You have it or you don't, but without it you're a washout. They'll give you a few names—Walter Winchell, Bernard Shaw, Orson Welles, Winston Churchill. Not very helpful to a mild and modest person who has no illusions about trailing clouds of glory. Besides, he may not like Winchell. Few persons seem to, though millions listen to him.

But Winchell has "flash," as do the others in their different ways. His voice is harsh with the rat-a-tat of drums, even repellent, and he dramatizes himself as the bearer of breath-taking news and gossip. He scorns the leisurely, informal conversational style and enters as though he were shouting from the housetops to warn you of a raid or a fire. Speed, drive, punch. You listen, even though you'd sometimes like to punch him. He is a son of a circus and has the showmanship that keeps the crowd openmouthed.

You see, Winchell has plenty of self-reliance. He doesn't wait for radiomen to tell him how to do it. He trusts himself and makes his own style. It may be that he gets his inspiration from Danton's, "Pour les vaincre, il nous faut de l'audace, encore de l'audace, et toujours de l'audace." (To conquer we must dare, and dare again, and always dare!)

Orson Welles has daring expressed in a cool inventiveness. As a novice he took to radio and moving pictures like a master and made the veteran directors sit around in disgust while he showed them how to do it. Shaw has the daring to tell his public what fools they are, and Churchill dared to face the worst with candor, dared to tell his people what they were up against, and dared to give them only "blood, sweat, and tears."

Showmanship is, in most respects, only another word for *personality*, but it may be greatly narrowed in application. One may not have all the accomplishments implied by personality. He may, indeed, have only one weapon with which to attack indifference, but it may be more than enough. There is the popular radio preacher, for instance, who develops his commonplace generalities through stories, anecdotes, personal experiences. "For instance" is a handy weapon to break down the dull abstractions that may creep into his talk. You see, a story has conflict and suspense. You simply must wait to see how it's coming out. And if it is a sad story about people who are worse off than you are, so much the better. That simple fact about human nature seems to account for the amazing success of John J. Anthony's Good Will Court.

At any rate, every radio director will insist that you dramatize your script with illustrations and examples. He is afraid you will get tiresome with explanation and argument. Listeners don't want to be educated. They want to be entertained, and you must practice the knack of making your information entertaining.

Of course, showmanship often refers to something in the voice. You must dare to be personal and escape from the boredom of the impersonal. You may be bitter and scornful, or indulgent and amused, or friendly and confidential— anything that shows your lively interest in your subject and indicates that you are not just another wooden declaimer or a schoolboy taking his lesson in reading aloud.

No one ever expects humor in the occasional radio address, and if you can get a smile or two you will be considered a wonder—a showman par excellence. If you can get off a nifty like Clare Boothe Luce's "globaloney," you are made. A college professor happened to say to his class, "Be a snob. Marry the boss's daughter." He at once became a high-priced writer for a newspaper syndicate and a featured radio speaker. It was as easy as that. Of course he had the talent to follow up his opportunities, but his offhand comedy was published and gave him his chance. Any genuine humor has the quality of unexpectedness, of surprise. It is daring, audacity in another form, even when it seems to be modest and disarming.

You may be one of those few persons who can qualify for that rare type of showmanship—that of telling the truth. We do not mean that speakers deliberately lie or willfully deceive. It is a fact, though, that they are seldom utterly sincere. They do not give the truth that is in them. They don't trust themselves. They echo what other people think and say. They give you what they think you want to hear, or what they think the best minds are thinking this year. And they give it to you in the language of their favorite books and magazines. Think of the harangues you listen to in the name of patriotism, pride, profit, prunes, and prisms. If you could only get an ounce of truth in that pound of palaver—a simple, direct, unadorned comment that searches your secret thoughts and touches your doubts, suspicions, and cynicisms!

On one of the afternoon network programs is a speaker who talks on the problems of life and conduct. He has no new answers—who has? But there is refreshing showmanship in his method and manner. He ad-libs—talks from notes—or gives a clever imitation of ad-libbing. He fumbles occasionally for a word, stalls a bit, like an acquaintance chatting with you. No public address stuff; just the relaxed, armchair offerings of a homespun philosopher who likes to talk things over with a sympathetic neighbor. He even puts in a plug for his sponsor without giving offense. And he's a better salesman than the usual announcer who reads the commercial. He says, in effect, "I wish you'd buy a can of so-and-so's soup. It's not bad; in fact, it's good, better than most popular brands. At any rate, if you'd like to have me around afternoons at this hour, remember that it's this soup that makes it possible." Now, that's honest talk, and the understatement of its advertising makes it highly persuasive.

Of course, there is something deceptive in this, too—deceptive in the sense that it isn't so simple and easy as it sounds. A man must be a fluent and sure speaker, or an actor who can read script with the effect intended.

For most of us there is only one safe rule, "Have something to say." The natural showman may get by with piffle but the ordinary man is like the salesman: he must sell himself first. He must believe sincerely and enthusiastically in his product before he can sell it to others. If you want to go on the radio just to show off to your friends, your talk will lack earnestness, the desire to convince or persuade. It will have no substantial purpose, no incentive to make it sharp and practical.

If you are representing some society, speaking for the Red Cross, or making the Jefferson anniversary address, don't depend on the respectable platitudes you've heard so often. They are true enough but very dull. Does the idea of Jefferson really stir you, or is he just a figurehead from another age to which you have to pay lip service? Just tossing off a lot of smart complimentary sentences won't get you anywhere.

The Red Cross is an old subject, too. It's been praised so much that many people don't want to hear any more about it. In fact, they'll tell you that there is too much money squandered on the Red Cross and that it's getting to be a racket. You know what prompts such thoughts and you have the chance to make a fine, eloquent talk, not by mouth-filling generalities, but by citing and describing some of the necessary things the Red Cross has done at home and abroad. You will show how the money is spent, how much more is needed. You will appeal to decency, generosity, sportsmanship, and will make the listener feel like a piker if he doesn't come through with something. In other words, you mean business. You're not talking just because you have to say something but because you have something to say.

When you prepare a talk around this core of thought and conviction, you'll get somewhere. You'll cut out the lah-de-dah drivel that is just filling up the required space and time. You'll get confidence and power and you'll read with gusto and enjoyment because you've "sold yourself on the idea" and are sure you have something interesting and profitable for the listening customer.

Showmanship is presenting your wares or ideas to advantage. All people like simplicity and color. Beyond that you have to remember that there are many publics, not just one. They have different tastes and interests. It is true that many intellectuals love baseball and prize fights, but one man's meat is still another man's poison. Don't try to please everybody. Follow your bent. Put life into your script and into your reading. What do we mean by life? That's right. You're learning. Don't be put off with vague and evasive words. It's not so easy to distinguish between the quick and the dead when it comes to language. Let's look at a few samples of showmanship now, before we tackle the chapters of details that follow.

Suppose you had only 5 minutes to say something stimulating to high-school students and young folks generally. You want to say something about courage, initiative, enterprise. You'd like to "pep" up your listeners into thinking that there are many good prizes in life and that they have the character to win them. You've got to make the race of life seem real, exciting, and near.

Several approaches might serve. You might use the sales manager's technique—shame them, show them what other salesmen have done, exhort them, urge them to get out there and fight.

You might be calmer and more objective, discuss jobs, how to approach employers, how to win good will, how to discover opportunities, how to use them promptly and effectively.

You might tell the story of someone you know, an ordinary chap no more gifted than the average, who worked and watched and made a success out of insignificant beginnings.

Mr. W. J. Cameron, who has had hundreds of thousands of listeners Sunday after Sunday on the Ford Sunday Evening Hour, had this problem and he chose to make his point by means of an analogy, a story that carried the central thought without much need of preachment. Mr. Cameron is himself a good example of the showmanship that grows out of thoughtful earnestness. Elocutionists would regard his voice as unsatisfactory. It is somewhat gravelly, tight, and tired. An occasional clearing of the throat does not help. But there is manly authority and conviction. It is a voice of experience. Mr. Cameron knows life. He knows there are no new ideas for the inspirational speaker to exploit. The fundamental principles are the same that Socrates, Plato, and their friends talked about. They are made appealing in every age, however, through fresh illustrations and constant reference to the familiar and intimate experience of listeners and readers.

Read this short speech and underline some of the specific items that make it dynamic. We'll say more about it later.

DON'T DIE ON THIRD

Tonight, the students of Greenfield Village and the Edison Institute are present as guests and participants in the program. Last year, on a similar occasion, we told a story. We shall attempt to tell a story—a true story—tonight.

It was twenty-five years ago, when the Detroit Tigers were playing the team from Cleveland. The score was a tie. It was the last half of the ninth, and two men were out. The fate of the game rested with Moriarty, the white-bloused figure that shuttled back and forth at third base. As the decisive moment approached, Tigers and Naps stood up at their benches, and eighteen thousand spectators bent forward in tense expectancy. Moriarty was on third.

He had come there in the ordinary way. At bat he had hit the ball and run to first. The next batter had bunted and sacrificed to move Moriarty on to second. Then a "long fly" had advanced him to third. There he stood, alert in every nerve, his powerful running legs, his quick eye, and quicker brain holding the hazard of the game.

Much as it meant to have advanced that far, third-base runs are not marked up on the scoreboard. Third base is not a destination—it is the last way station on the road "home." The world is full of third bases. To leave school, to earn your college degree, to enter a profession, is only to start toward third base. To get the job you want, even to become the head of your business, is merely to reach third base. Third base is opportunity,

and opportunity is not arrival, it is only another point of depar-
ture. Attain the White House itself, and you have got only as
far as third base. The test of all you have is yet to come. No
time for self-applause at third—many a promising run has died
there. And there stood Moriarty. If he failed, it was not alone;
the team failed with him. Concentrated on him at that moment
were the hopes and fears of thousands who seemed to hold their
breath, and so still was the great park that even the breeze seemed
forgetful to blow.

One way to get off third is to wait for someone to bat you off.
Another is to get away on your own initiative—Moriarty chose
that. He knew his game. He knew the catcher's signals called
for a ball thrown high to Mullin, who was now at bat. He knew
that a runner might duck low to touch the home plate while the
catcher's mitt was in the air for a high ball. He knew that in
throwing high, pitchers "wind up" in a certain way. He knew
also that pitchers have a way of "winding up" when they don't
intend to throw. He knew, moreover, that this pitcher, being
left-handed, could not keep watch on third while delivering the
ball—the runner might safely take a longer lead. Moriarty
knew all the ins and outs of his job. Luck might lie in the lap
of the gods, but preparation, knowledge, judgment, and initiative
were with the player.

Had Moriarty waited for Mullin to bat, Mullin might have
failed him, ending the inning. One opening remained: make
"home" between the moment the pitch was begun past all recall
and the moment the ball struck the catcher's mitt—make "home"
in the fraction of time Mullin's hit or miss hung in futurity. That
would be a contest in speed between a 5-ounce ball delivered
with all the force of a superb pitching arm and the 170-pound
body of Moriarty! An unequal contest, for the pitched ball
travels only 60 feet while the runner from third must hurl his body
over a distance of 90 feet.

Moriarty is on third. He builds his prospective run as an
engineer builds a bridge across a torrent, with infinite pains.
Now the Cleveland pitcher is poising himself for a throw. Mori-

arty is crouched like a tiger ready to spring—now! There is a white streak across the field! A cloud of dust at the home plate! The umpire stands over it with hands extended, palms down. The baseball park echoes and reechoes with a thunderous roar of acclaim, which bursts forth again and again in thrilling electric power. Every eye strains toward the man who is slapping the dust from his white uniform. Moriarty is home!

It was only a run made in the course of a baseball game; but it has been saying to us these many years—Don't die on third. You may be put out, but it need not be by your inaction. If the run must die, let it die trying. All of us are on bases. Some of us are waiting for someone to bat us farther. Suppose he misses! Mullin missed the ball that day—had Moriarty waited, he would not have scored. It would not be right to say that all the world's a baseball diamond—it does offer us the ever-present choice between indolence and initiative, but life's rules are fairer. In life there is an inner scoreboard where every effort is credited to your record. Many a valiant run is lost, but the valor of it builds the soul. So, while there's one thing yet to do, or a fraction of time to do it in, don't die on third. Study conditions, learn all you can, use all you learn, summon your strength and courage, defy luck—and then, bold player—just by doing this, you have already scored. Something great is strengthened within you. The run may fail, but you have not, and there's another game tomorrow.

How neatly, and yet not too long, the speaker holds Moriarty at third base while he delivers a one-paragraph sermon and reminds you that all success is only getting to third, and that you should not take time out for self-applause.

In the next paragraph you get the detailed inside knowledge of the game. The speaker has proved himself, won his audience with this realistic know-how, and revealed the idea that grew into a speech: "Moriarty knew all the ins and outs of his job. Luck might be in the lap of the gods, but preparation, knowledge, judgment, and initiative were with the player."

Note again the closing idea, in the last paragraph. "In life there is an inner scoreboard where every effort is credited to your record. Many a valiant run is lost, but the valor of it builds the soul." All's right in the world, young people, if you have courage and persistence.

The customers want action and Mr. Cameron gives it to them. He whisks over his own commercial, his little homily, while the pitcher is winding up, and gets in an eloquent "so-what" while Moriarty is still dusting off his uniform after his brilliant steal and slide. That's great timing and great showmanship.

Some people think Mr. Cameron is a bit old-fashioned in style and preachment, but it's a mistake to be dogmatic about such things. Successful writers and speakers disclose a variety that should not be superficially classified and labeled.

We should, however, be aware of differences in rhythm, in sentence structure, in choice of words—in the atmosphere that a speaker creates. To illustrate a quite different style from that of Mr. Cameron we are giving you now a speech by a country editor whose business philosophy is, we believe, fundamentally the same as Mr. Cameron's. The talk was delivered on America's Town Meeting of the Air, August 6, 1942. The subject was "The Role of the Press in Wartime." We quote from the *Town Meeting Bulletin*,[1] beginning with the moderator's introduction of Mr. Lewis.

MODERATOR DENNY: There are from five to six thousand weekly newspapers throughout America, and millions of Americans

[1] Reprinted from *Town Meeting Bulletin*, Vol. 8, No. 15, official transcript of America's Town Meeting of the Air, published by American Education Press, Inc., Columbus, Ohio.

depend upon them as the sources of their news and information. Mr. Sol Lewis, editor of *The Lynden Tribune*, speaks for the weekly paper. Mr. Lewis. (*Applause.*)

MR. LEWIS: Neighbors, I am batting for the small-town newspapers in this discussion and I can bunt out only a few rural thoughts. On rhubarb and gooseberries, for instance. I never liked 'em in normal times. With sugar limited now, suffering among rhubarb and gooseberry consumers must be terrific. (*Applause.*)

Now that the thought of this has your expression well puckered, I want to point out to you that it is my belief that the major policy of the press in wartime should be to battle the Rhubarb Regiments and Gooseberry Guards throughout America—the sour souls who are flooding us with tears and pessimism and nasty whispers. Put these Bawl Babies back in their cribs!

Drown out their wails with booming facts about American courage, American resources, and American production. I've been through the amazing Boeing plant right here in Seattle. I've seen the Flying Fortresses zip through on the assembly lines at the lightning speed that American mechanical wizards have made possible. Each gigantic plane provides an editorial argument that should silence that Rhubarb Regiment, exactly as its huge bomb load can silence the Japs.

Let the American press stand up on its hind legs and cheer for the Army and Navy—they'll never be licked. Cheer for our Yankee Commander in Chief and our Yankee Congress. We, the people of the United States, authorize them to run this war for us. Sure, they're making plenty of mistakes. But if our business were increased a hundredfold overnight and we had to employ a lot of green hands, we'd have plenty of weevils with wormy ideas on our editorial staffs, too (*laughter*), and it might take us a few days to stamp 'em out. Give the President and his aides a little time, and we'll all be going places. Yes, and Berlin and Tokyo will be included in our itinerary.

Now, I don't mean that our readers be kept in a rose-colored Aleutian fog, and that the news of defeats and discouragements and dishonesty in war administration should be withheld. But let such dismal information be kept in its proper place, which is subordinate to the major tale of significant achievements in the air and on the sea and in our American factories and shipyards, achievements that are leading to ultimate victory.

I wish that the press could ration out to the readers with the gasoline jitters some of the soothing horse sense of our peaceful country towns. The public is nervous. Calm 'em down. When my son, Bill, was five, he was afraid of the little crabs, while wading. I made a few scratches on the buckle of his swimming belt and told Bill they read, "Crabs, keep away!" Bill felt safe. He couldn't read, and neither could the crabs. (*Laughter.*)

Editors ought to realize that there has been a great change in the reading public since the outbreak of the war. The young men, the hale and hearty, have gone to the camps. Yes, and the restrictions have been lifted, so that the sway-backed and popeyed are being taken, too. (*Laughter.*) Who are left besides the women and children? Just the nervous, crabby old folks, the physically and mentally defective, and the married men. (*Laughter.*) Surely editorial policies should be changed to take care of this subscription list of the halt and the blind and the babes. They should be comforted and cheered. Yet I find that three out of five of the comics syndicated for the youngsters now deal with the war. Comics? Just as funny as coffins. (*Laughter.*)

Let the press campaign for more reading. Praise learning and research. Encourage boys and girls to look up to such of our greatest Americans as George Washington Carver, former slave, the fine old Negro scientist. Glorify sound, simple virtues in place of featuring dollars, fashions, glamour girls, and heiresses in slacks. Clamor for the simple times of old, when we wore britches and we didn't get too big for 'em.

How the press should conduct itself in wartime ought to be determined by how we want the public to conduct itself in wartime. We want the people working intelligently, loyally, enthusiastically. We don't want them distracted and disturbed by extras and alarms every hour. Let the press give them the

facts, interpret the facts soberly, and instill faith in the doctors
we have in charge of the case during this emergency.   I recall
going through a similar critical situation personally.   I put
complete trust in the physician.   I didn't idle around waiting for
bulletins.   I worked doubly hard.   I felt I had to.   I was
scared.   I thought we might have triplets.   (*Laughter.*)

Well, it's a real privilege to present these meandering country
views as my part in this nail-keg discussion.   We don't have such
forums in our country stores any more.   Believe me, Mr. Denny,
it takes a mighty low priority number these days even to sit on a
nail keg.   (*Applause.*)

You don't have to be told that this is good showmanship.
The small-town atmosphere is spread deliberately.   Beginning with "Neighbors," Mr. Lewis hands out the homespun
with something of the drollery of Will Rogers.   See what a
few simple words can do—*rhubarb, gooseberries, weevils,
britches, nail kegs.*   Mr. Lewis avoids going literary (he even
slices *them* to *'em*), but he is eloquent as well as humorous.
The eloquence is all the more effective because it is so disarming, so simply put.

Notice that the fun in this speech is not a collection of
"funny" stories.   It consists of analogies, similes, situations,
name calling, and whimsical comment.   "Comics? Just
as funny as coffins."   The next to the last paragraph is a
gorgeous piece of deception—an apparently serious comparison of the public's war jitters with Mr. Lewis's personal
crisis.   We suffer with him until the uproarious anticlimax.
Mark Twain couldn't have done it better.

Well, it's time that we got to the business of showing how
you can make your own talks convincing and compelling.

CHAPTER III

The Strategy of the Radio Speech

Not long ago a prominent businessman was addressing sales managers on the problem of how to increase production. He said, "Warfare is composed of three major elements: Strategy is the planning of warfare. Tactics is the execution of those plans. Logistics, the third branch of military science, is the supplying of everything necessary to strategy and tactics—in the right amount, at the right place, at the right time."

Now, public speaking is a good deal like that. You are trying to subdue indifference, disagreement, hostility. You are trying to capture the minds and hearts of listeners who may tune you out at any moment to seek the siren charms of a singer, an orchestra, or another speaker. You, too, must consider strategy, tactics, and logistics.

Strategy, in speaking, aims at getting the right response. You are talking for some purpose and that purpose is not merely to be interesting. Your objective is not achieved if the response is,

"Yes, I enjoyed it, but so what?"   Or

"It was amusing, but it didn't get anywhere."   Or

"It's a nice pipe dream, but it can't come true. Just another half-baked idealist."   Or

"Yes, it's true enough, but everybody knows all that." Or

"It's too complicated; I can't understand it."   Or

"I'm not spending money on that.   It doesn't amount to much.   What with war bonds, taxes, and the rest, that fellow has a nerve to ask me to shell out for his racket."   Or

"That's no argument at all.   He must think we're pretty dumb.   Nothing but a few wisecracks.   No point to the thing."

Every talk produces some sort of response, but too often it is not the response desired by the speaker.   And the reason is that the speaker has not thought specifically enough about the response he wishes to get.   He has no definite focus, no particular point of view, no one significant thought he wants his listeners to retain.

The textbooks on speaking are always reminding us that there are certain general ends or purposes of speech, and that we should carefully decide which one will be the most strategically useful in operations upon audience interest. The teacher, for instance, has the general purpose of *giving information* or imparting skill.   He gets his desired response when the student says, "I understand" or "I can do it."

The lecturer who speaks on Alexander Hamilton wants to *impress* his hearers with the character and the contributions of the statesman to American welfare.   He interprets facts already known and makes them more vivid, realistic, and meaningful.   The response should be something like this, "I never realized before how necessary and how valuable the work of Hamilton was.   I was inclined to regard him as a reactionary who didn't have the faith in democracy that his great rival Jefferson had."

The third purpose is to *win belief*.   A large part of talk consists of argument, of trying to convince people that such and such is the right thing to believe or to do.   The response, when it is satisfactory, will include a confession of ignorance or oversight, such as, "I hadn't thought of that.

I was hasty and maybe prejudiced. There's more to it than I realized. This fellow seems to know his onions. Nice chap, too. He made one point I'll have to spring on the boys in the office tomorrow."

A fourth general end is to *persuade*, to get people to do something—to buy your product, to vote for your candidate, to give to some worthy cause. Persuasion often by-passes logic and appeals directly to desire and sentiment. The good salesman makes people want things so much that they will make their own arguments—often pretty flimsy—to satisfy their consciences for spending money extravagantly.

A fifth purpose is to *entertain*, to get a few laughs, to offer curiosities and novelties that will give escape from the familiar commonplaces and routines. Story, anecdote, drama help to project all the other purposes more securely.

Though several of these purposes may appear in a single talk, they should support the one chief purpose and should not distract attention from it. Let us suppose that you have made a considerable study of Russia and intend to give a talk about that country. Now, Russia is a big area, like banking, advertising, or the New Deal. You can't treat the whole subject in 15 or 30 minutes. Your problem of strategy is to select material most profitable for your limited time. The you-attitude will help you solve it. What questions about Russia are uppermost in the minds of your audience today? Do they want to know what difference it makes that the Comintern is dissolved? Are they worrying whether Russia will fight Japan? Do they fear that the whole of Europe will go communistic? Would they enjoy human-interest stories about the Russian generals?

You will, of course, consider your own limitations. You are better equipped to make a good talk about some aspects of your subject than about others, but you do what you can to strike directly at vital interests in your audience. You make up your mind where to attack. You put down on paper your objective, the response you want:

"I want this audience to realize that Russia can't be beaten." Or

"Russia will take part in the war against Japan." Or

"Be assured that Russia will not be a threat after Allied victory."

Let's examine another subject, one that was discussed on America's Town Meeting of the Air, July 23, 1942—"Will War Marriages Work?" The Town Meeting likes conflicting opinion on controversial issues and assigns speakers on opposing sides to get some dramatic head-on collisions. Fun for the audience if not for the speakers. But experienced speakers know better than to get too far out on the limb of dogmatic argument. They say "yes" and "no," but mostly one or the other.

The speaker may be asked to stay definitely on the side allotted him because it is his preference, but he still has a problem of strategy. He wishes to avoid a contentious attitude and stay pleasantly relaxed. He will agree with his opponent as far as he can and still make his difference of opinion firm and convincing. A touch of humor will relieve tension and disarm hostility.

So we find Lewis Browne doing a little clowning with a subject that invites it. He also reveals his strategy. "I'd be a fool to try to argue that they are the best kind. War marriages! Don't feel too elated, Mr. Seabury. (*Laughter.*) I'm not surrendering—I'm merely beating a strategic retreat. In the language of the communiques, I'm withdrawing to a position 'previously prepared' and, believe me, it's a strong one." (*Laughter.*)

And this is it, as summarized in the last paragraph of his talk. "The whole issue, therefore, comes down to this: Will war marriages work? The answer is no and yes. No, they probably won't work so well as ordinary marriages. Yes, they certainly will work a lot better than no marriages." Somehow, Mr. Browne manages to have his cake and eat it too.

David Seabury is more downright and decisive with his "no." He begins with the statement that only about 10 per cent of all marriages work well and adds, a little later, "If few peacetime marriages remain happy, what are these hurried hurtlings into wedlock going to be like?" As a consulting psychiatrist, Mr. Seabury had plenty of experience in observing the results of marriages in the last war and can cite many unfavorable cases.

But marriage is hardly a question of logic, and the philosopher and the psychologist, though interesting, are inconclusive. At the end of the question period Mr. Browne has the last comment and probably steals the show. He says, "I can't help adding just this thing. If they are fighting for us because we made mistakes and if we were such fools that we could make such mistakes, how dare we arrogate to ourselves the right to say to them what they shall do?" (*Applause*.)

With the kind permission of Town Meeting[1] we are reprinting the speeches referred to. Study the strategy and the plan of each. The academic and the practical meet, and sometimes the academic seems more practical than the practical, if you know what we mean.

[1] Reprinted from *Town Meeting Bulletin*, Vol. 8, No. 13, official transcript of America's Town Meeting of the Air, published by American Education Press, Inc., Columbus, Ohio.

MR. BROWN: Mr. Denny, ladies, and gentlemen. To ask whether war marriages will work is precisely like asking whether retreaded tires will work. Obviously, such tires won't work as well as new ones. They'll wear out sooner, they'll blow out oftener, and they'll cause anxiety almost all of the time. (*Laughter.*) But what can we do? New tires just aren't available, so we've got to put up with retreaded ones, if we are lucky enough to get them. From now on until the return of peace, it's either retreaded tires or no tires.

Similarly, with regard to marriage. I'd be a fool to try to argue that they are the best kind. War marriages! Don't feel too elated, Mr. Seabury. (*Laughter.*) I'm not surrendering—I'm merely beating a strategic retreat. In the language of the communiques, I'm withdrawing to a position "previously prepared," and, believe me, it's a strong one. (*Laughter.*)

Yes, I willingly concede that war marriages are far from ideal. To be that, they would have to be made in heaven; but instead, they are contracted in war, which is, as you know, hell. (*Laughter.*) Yet what would you have us do? Pass laws restricting marriage for the duration? Impossible. You can't ration passion. (*Loud laughter and applause.*) No, from now until the return of peace, it's either war marriages—or war marriages. (*Laughter.*)

I confess that I, myself, did not realize this until just a little while ago. The fact was brought home to me during a recent lecture tour when I chanced to address a large girls' college in Texas. My subject was the war. But when the discussion period ensued, almost the first question was about marriage. Was that a natural association of ideas? Well, a young lady arose to inquire whether I was in favor of war marriages, and almost without thinking, I answered, "No."

Whereupon, after a moment of deafening silence, another young woman rose up and asked, "But didn't you just say, Mr. Browne, that this war will probably last several years?" "Yes," I admitted. "Then, what are we girls going to do?" she went on. "Many of us are already in our twenties, and if we wait several

years, we may never get married." She had me there. For
the life of me, I couldn't think of an adequate answer. I hope
Mr. Seabury can.

I may sound facetious, but I actually am in deep earnest.
Consider the plight of that young woman. She is one of millions
who are going to college, or working in factories, or clerking in
stores, or perhaps developing bunions at USO dances. (*Laughter.*) But she has no intention of doing that the rest of her life.
She's healthy, she's normal, which means she wants to become a
wife, and—within limits—a mother. But for some reason or
another she neglected to secure a priority on a man. (*Laughter.*)
She has no childhood sweetheart; so if she's going to marry at all,
it must be to someone whom she has just met.

Now, what shall she do? Shall she make sure first that he is
ineligible for the draft? But if he's that sort of man, the chances
are that he is ineligible for marriage, too. He must be blind in
more than one eye (*laughter*), and deaf in more than one ear
(*laughter*), or old enough to have more than a dozen grandchildren.
So she's stuck. She wants, and she certainly deserves, a chap who
is A-1, and if he's that, he's probably in 1-A. (*Laughter.*)

Now, let us suppose that she has encountered such a young man.
In normal times she would be able to "keep company" with him
for months, before making up her mind to make up his mind.
(*Laughter.*) And that would be good. People who are careful to
marry at leisure are less likely to get divorced in haste. But these
aren't normal times. If she hesitates now she is lost, for that
young man is here today and gone tomorrow. So she doesn't
hesitate.

Can you blame her? She realizes that if she insists on putting
off marriage until he returns, she runs the risk of putting it off
forever, for he will return to find her older—perhaps several years
older. Of course, he too will be older, but being a male he won't
feel older. (*Laughter and applause.*) Consequently, he will
probably find her younger sister more attractive.

So can you blame our poor heroine, therefore, if she throws
caution to the winds? And can you blame the young hero if he

helps her throw it there? After all, he too feels that he cannot afford to dally. In the good old days—normal times—he could dare to postpone proposing until the advent of what the lady novelists used to call the "psychological moment." But these aren't normal times, and the psychological moment has become the biological moment. Deplorable? Of course, that is deplorable. But so is everything else connected with war. The whole thing is a bloody mess.

The fact remains, however, that the war is here and that we must see it through. On the whole, I am inclined to believe that young people who are married will be able to see it through more sanely—certainly more soberly—than those who remain single.

Take the case of the man. Now, if he were a hired soldier, a mercenary, it would, no doubt, be an advantage to keep him single. But in our Army, he is a citizen. He fights for his country, not for sport or for loot. The surest way, therefore, of making him fight well is to give him a stake in his country; and what stronger stake is there than a wife and the thought of little ones? And even if a marriage does not make him fight better, at least it makes him live better. It gives him a sense of responsibility. It helps to keep him steady—or at least a little less unsteady.

What little experience I have had lately as a civilian lecturer for the War Department has left me utterly convinced that married soldiers are by and large far more dependable, or shall I say less undependable, than unmarried ones.

And what is true for a man is equally true for a woman. If he needs a stake in the country, she needs a stake in the war. She has to feel that it is her war, otherwise she will be less inclined to do her utmost to help win it. Therefore, marriage to someone in the service almost necessarily arouses her to greater war activity.

The other day I was talking to a woman welder in one of the aircraft plants down in Santa Monica. She said to me, "When I weld 'em, I weld 'em good. My John's over in Australia, and I say to myself, 'Who knows, maybe this plane I'm welding is just the one they're going to put him in when they ferry him over to

Java or to Japan.' " And with a thought like that in her mind, you can bet on it that she does weld them good.

Finally, there is this to be considered. Marriage is advantageous not alone because it gives the young man a stake in the country and the young woman a stake in the war, but also because it gives the Nation a stake in the future. Marriage brings forth children. To be sure, mere mating does too—just ordinary barnyard or stud-farm mating such as we are told is being encouraged over in Nazi Germany. But who among us would favor that? No, we want children born in decent and responsible wedlock. And we can't have them—we can't begin to have nearly enough of them—if we keep these millions of our young people cramped in single cussedness until peace returns—this war is over.

I ask you, Mr. Seabury, since you're taking the opposite side, isn't that true? How in the world are we going to keep up mass reproduction with all the mess production there is around? We've got to have young ones. Our future depends upon them; and if we're going to take this whole segment of the population— the youthful, the fertile, the fecund population—out of marriage entirely, or almost entirely, what chance is there for our future? We'll win the war and leave no one to enjoy the victory.

No. The whole issue, therefore, comes down to this: Will war marriages work? The answer is no and yes. No, they probably won't work so well as ordinary marriages. Yes, they certainly will work a lot better than no marriages. (*Applause.*)

MODERATOR DENNY: Thank you, Mr. Browne.

That's a pretty sharp barrage you fired in the direction of David Seabury, but let's see what this eminent consulting psychologist has to say about his twenty years' experience in New York City. David Seabury, fire away. (*Applause.*)

MR. SEABURY: I appreciate the optimistic spirit of my opponent tonight. In this unbelieving world it takes courage to trust in the cause for which he battles. I, too, would like to think that all marriages—war marriages especially—should be made in heaven. I'll go further. I'd like to install a Lewis Browne on every street corner, dressed as Cupid, to see that each unmarried boy finds his perfect girl. (*Laughter.*) In fact, I would like to make a law prohibiting unhappiness in marriage so Cupid Browne could spend the rest of his days blessing couple after couple as they march into endless bliss.

But isn't there something wrong with this picture? I fear it is not a dream but a nightmare. If truth must be told, only about 10 per cent of all marriages work well; and for the rest, the husband works, and the wife works, they work each other, but they seldom make the marriage work. So I hope the title of our discussion tonight does not imply that marriage made in peacetime is always blessed by billing and cooing. Boy meets girl in good periods and bad. And marriage isn't blissful just because nations are not at war.

After all, the whole question of matrimony is a serious issue. There is, in fact, a direct relation between the causes of war among nations and a war between individuals. If you could count the number of quarreling couples in the world, see the broken homes and the upset neighborhoods they create, you would discover where war starts. Peace, if it comes, must begin in the home.

And remember this, safety for the state depends upon marriage, for marriage makes the home, the home produces the children who become its future citizens. Lower the standard of marriage, and you lower the life of the nation. In some measure, that is what is already happening. There has been a 215 per cent increase in divorce in this country since the year 1900. By 1930, two out of every nine marriages ended in divorce, and, as Mr. Denny told you, it is now two out of every seven. If countless hasty marriages are made, every young couple will be in the divorce courts by 1955.

Now, I'd like to believe that we were also thinking of marriage for the sake of the children. Mr. Browne touched upon that point. I know from years of experience that there is no environment in the world that produces a worse citizen, or a more sick citizen, or a more neurotic citizen, than a broken home. We don't want a country full of people who have been shocked by the turmoil and quarreling that can exist in a home.

We ask, then, "Will war marriages work?" and I'd like to ask, "Will any marriage work, unless it is founded on full acquaintanceship and real love?"

There are, unfortunately, seven kinds of attraction that produce marriage nowadays. Real devotion is, of course, the only important one—that sense of having found a partner to whom you can give yourself utterly. Then comes romancing, the sort of falling in love with love, which makes one imagine the sweetheart is perfect. What we call erotic love comes next, but it won't make a permanent relation. There needs to be spiritual and intellectual concord as well. Yet mere mental harmony isn't enough. That is why plenty of friendships become bad marriages. It is also why the fifth form—marrying for home and children—works only with cold and selfish natures. Love is then given for what the partner does, not for what the partner is. I've seen more tragedy come because of marriage for home and children without a real devotion between the two individuals. That's the point we need to remember whether we're in peace or war. Marriage because you are thrown together; that's the kind of thing where they both like peanuts, they're both P. D.'s (they're both perfect dancers)—they can get married. They have no idea of whether they can live together. Or marriage to escape being single is equally unsuccessful.

Only if those wonderful words in the wedding ceremony, "to become one flesh," have taken place, will marriage produce a permanent happiness. And such a union may happen at any time, in times of war as well as in times of peace.

When we speak of a war marriage, therefore, we do not mean a marriage that would have come to pass anyway, but only one that has been hurried up by the war and in large measure caused by it. You know how it is. It usually takes—and Mr. Browne touched upon this point—six weeks for a girl to get the boy to propose, and six months before she tells him when the wedding date is to be. That gives her time to look him over.

Now, it is different with a war marriage. He is in uniform. He is serving his country. That stirs him deeply. He stirs each girl he meets. She is in no mood to consider what he is like. She doesn't ask herself if she can live with him for years. She doesn't even imagine how he will dance after he has eighty more pounds about his middle. She only thinks of how he dances now. That is what we mean by a war marriage, one made in the moment, for the moment, without stopping to think of the years to come. If few peacetime marriages remain happy, what are these hurried hurtlings into wedlock going to be like?

That's the sort of thing we need to realize, for I know how you feel. It isn't fair to ask you to put off marrying. It isn't fair to make youth pay for our adult mishandling of the world that permitted another war. I admit it is cruel, but not half so cruel as to fling youth into a bad marriage.

I wish with all my heart I could believe that war marriages would work. I don't want youth deprived of love. I don't want their romance delayed. I hate this brutal conflict that challenges their right to each other. I hate even to suggest that after they find each other everything won't be perfect. But I know life. I have had to face it in the despair of thousands. I appreciate, too, why youth says, "Let me have a little happiness now, and I'll risk the future." But is the risk of a few years, a few weeks of joy, worth the gamble of years of suffering? I doubt it. Sherman told us war is hell. I'll tell you an unhappy marriage is war. You can add his epithet if you want.

In my capacity as a consulting psychologist I have had to bind up the wounds of many of those who made hurried marriages in the last war, and I know that not more than 5 per cent of those marriages remained happy. Here are some of the common complaints of war brides after the husbands returned. First, "I find it hard to get acquainted with him; he doesn't seem to know me as he did before he went away." Second, "He isn't sure he loves me; he wants to dance with lots of other girls." And third, "He's awfully rough with me, and he swears like everything." Fourth, "He doesn't want children now; he says he wants to play for a while, and he talks about the girls who said 'Oo-la-la' every time he smiled. He wants me to admire him as if I were a whole street full of people watching him parade." And lastly she says, "He has changed and I have changed; I didn't think we would."

And here are the complaints of soldier-husbands after their return. "Gee, I don't want to be a bundle-toter right off the bat." And second, "Gosh, you can't ask a fellow to take orders from a wife after the discipline he has had." "Mother says she wants me back home for a while, and after all a fellow only has one mother." "Say, why is making love to a wife so different from making love to a sweetheart?" "I thought I'd get back home for the sort of chow mother used to make, but Susie can't fry an egg." "Have I got to pay alimony all my life for three weeks' marriage?" And lastly, "I wasn't shell-shocked over there. I got mine when I saw my wife." (*Laughter.*)

Now, if you can squeeze out of remarks like those the feeling that war marriages work, you're a lot smarter than I am. And I ask you to note these next three points, namely: The time of a soldier's return is a period of great adjustment for him; second, the end of a war is a period of great readjustment for the world about him; third, the first year of married life under the same roof is notoriously difficult for two young people.

Now, when the average man in times of peace and prosperity makes a poor go of the first year of marriage, how can a soldier full of emotional turmoil, and aggravated by economic pressure, return to marriage with a wife who is half a stranger to him? Would not both young people do better to hold to their love rather than to make it into a marriage at such a time?

Lovers can keep their devotion and maintain their love even if he is in a far country and she at home. They can seek glory in their faithfulness to love. They can accept this war as a proving time of the reality of their love. Every great romance throughout history gains its inimitable power from the love that endured a time of trial and stress.   The great love story is great because of the courage it reveals to keep and to protect love without any possessive demands upon the sweetheart.

And let us never forget that a war marriage does not ensure love. It may destroy the greatest chance that will ever come to youth to prove its heroism and its faith.   I only ask you to respect love and not to marry without daring to give love the test life is offering, the test that proves its greatness and theirs.   (*Applause.*)

CHAPTER IV
Tactics in Organizing Your Talk

You have spent some time in selecting the object of your speech before you choose the exact subject. You know what you are about. The next problem is to put over the idea effectively, to get people to listen, and to stay with your broadcast to the end.

In every talk you are a salesman. You have to answer questions like these:

Why should I listen to this?

What is there in this for me?

Why not get down to brass tacks?

Are you another college professor? You sound a bit screwy.

Will it work? Has anybody tried it? Where?

Why is it better than what we've got now?

Won't it cost too much?

Isn't it just more of my money for bureaucrats to toss away?

How does it cut down expenses?

What can I do about it?

You've heard your English teachers talk about unity, coherence, and emphasis—a triple threat for many students. But it's only an academic statement of common sense.

Unity is keeping your eye on the ball—and this isn't football. Don't hide the ball from your listeners. Don't give them so many distracting or diverting ideas that they lose sight of your principal point and fail to respond as you planned.

Coherence is simply clearness—developing your material in a natural and orderly fashion. It implies short sentences easy to speak and easy to comprehend, a conversational rhythm that allows the listener comfortable participation in the thought and mood.

Emphasis takes you back to more awareness of plan. Should you state your central thought at once, or wait until you have removed objections or created interest? Should you summarize the thought at the end of your talk, close with an impressive incident, or urge some kind of action?

Emphasis is frequently a matter of position. Your first words appeal to curiosity, your last may be remembered longest. In platform speaking, a talk may remind you of the shape of an orange. You may begin mildly, swell to vigorous description, explanation, and climax, and diminish to a swift and tranquil close.

But the radio talk puts more pressure on the speaker. Every sentence must sustain interest. A slow beginning is fatal. Your audience will leave for more excitement elsewhere. A tame ending may give a sense of time wasted. And yet no part of the talk should sound strained, artificial, or overeager. The language and the tone should reflect sincerity, ease, and poise.

Every talk may be organized around the framework of beginning, discussion, and ending. In the order of preparation, however, it may be best to give your attention first to the meat of your talk, the discussion. Jot down the items that seem necessary and relevant. As you ponder them, you will leave out some and add others. You may spend some time rearranging the order of topics before you find the most effective sequence, especially if you are explaining or arguing. In a narrative or story you simply put things in the order in which they happened.

Your first jottings may be meager. You may feel that you can tell the whole thing in a paragraph. And so you can. But that is only the abstract or plot of your talk. It is a skeleton that needs flesh and blood—the life that comes with comparison and contrast, cause and effect, details, explanations, illustrations and examples—the emphasis that grows in expanding a generality by means of a specific instance.

You probe your subject and subtopics with questions. You know how Kipling managed to get on with his writing:

> I keep six honest serving-men
> (They taught me all I knew);
> Their names are What and Why and When
> And How and Where and Who.

Remember the sign in the stores. You meet it on the way out, "Have you forgotten anything?" You may forget the most telling and decisive fact or proof or example or clarifying detail unless you discover the questions an audience would like to ask you. These, in turn, will prompt you to ask other questions about the extent and use of your material.

As for making the best plan for presenting your unassorted and somewhat scrambled topics, the advice of Lyman Abbott, reprinted years ago in Brander Matthews' *Notes on Public Speaking*, is as practical for the radio age as it was for the horse-and-buggy oratorical era. He said:

> In special preparation, [there are] five successive steps: (1) What is the object of this speech? What end is it to serve? What verdict is it to win? What result is it to accomplish? (2) Central thought. What thought lodged in the mind of an auditor will

best accomplish the desired result? (3) Analysis of this central thought into three or four propositions, the enforcement and illustration of which will serve to fasten in the minds of the hearers the central thought, and to secure the desired result. (4) Some illustrations or concrete statements of each of these separate propositions. (5) These four points firmly fixed in the mind; then an endeavor on these lines of thought to win this result with this audience, exactly as one would endeavor to win assent from an individual.

Notice those last words—"exactly as one would endeavor to win assent from an individual." What could be more timely? Abbott understood, better than most speakers of his day, the importance of talking to and with his audience and not at it. He would have recommended that you discuss your subject with one or two interested listeners before you start writing the speech.

Vital Speeches of June 1, 1943, has a talk which Dr. D. F. Fleming broadcast over station WSM, Nashville, Tenn. We take the liberty of reprinting it here because it illustrates so well the tactics of organization. First, note the outline which we have made by simply following the order of the topics as they appear.

SHALL THE HULL METHOD OF TARIFF MAKING BE ENDED?

Beginning.
  I. Subject may sound dull but it is important to you.
  II. Congress must decide before June 12 whether to continue trade agreements.
Discussion.
  I. Failure to continue would be sign of isolationism and nationalism.
    A. Combination of local interests in Congress could defeat renewal of trade agreements.

    B. Tariff not so disastrous when we were a debtor nation.

II. The way the new method of tariff making works.

    A. Meetings of experts who submit lists of commodities in question.

    B. Special committees bargain about exports and imports.

    C. Final result is a delicate balance of compromises.

    D. So far, our exports have greatly exceeded our imports.

    E. No home producers have been seriously hurt.

III. Comparison of negotiated agreements with the old method of tariff making.

    A. Crush of petitioners for protection appeared before House Ways and Means Committee.

    B. Proceedings were a notorious failure because of inadequate time allowed.

    C. 531 laymen elected to Congress can only make chaotic guesses, usually too high, about tariff rates.

    D. The Hull method is deliberate, careful, and continuous.

        1. Men with great knowledge of trade conditions weigh evidence for each proposed change.

IV. One dangerous objection made to the Hull method.

    A. Trade agreement said to be treaties and subject to Senate approval.

        1. One-third of senators could defeat trade agreements.

V. Tariff is too complicated for Congress.

    A. Logrolling always results in special tariff favors.

Ending.

    I. This is no time to revert to economic war.

    II. We are not required to play Santa Claus but we must buy as well as sell.

    III. To kill the trade agreements now would give a death blow to hopes of organizing nations against future wars.

This may sound like a dull subject, but I believe I can convince you that it intimately affects our future peace and happiness.

Before June 12 the Congress must decide whether or not to continue the Hull method of making tariffs by negotiated agree-

ments with other nations.   This authority has been given to Mr.
Hull three times since 1934 for a period of three years each time.
In these nine years agreements have been negotiated with twenty-
seven nations, including one with Iran, or Persia, signed only on
April 8.   All of these agreements will expire soon, unless the
authority behind them is renewed.

Failure to continue this friendly, give-and-take method of
making tariffs would unquestionably be taken by the rest of the
world as a sure sign that the United States is headed back into
another period of isolationism and extreme nationalism.   The
notice would be so clear that no one could possibly misunderstand
it.   Failure to renew the trade agreements might not seem to us
to be a declaration of war but it would be interpreted abroad as
something close to that—economic war in the postwar period and
a third world war at the end of that road.

The renewal of the trade agreements could nevertheless be
defeated by a combination in Congress of local interests, each of
which wanted high tariff protection for itself, regardless of the
effect upon the nation as a whole, and upon other nations.   In
the past, tariff laws have been made mainly by this method.   The
result was not always disastrous in a period when we were a debtor
nation and when peace depended less on peaceful trade, but in the
future we dare not leave out of account the effects of our tariffs
upon the national welfare and upon the welfare of other
nations.

The new method of tariff making enables the national interest
to be considered.   It works something like this: after preliminary
negotiation has established the possibility of an agreement with
Iran, let us say, the government of Iran will send to this country a
delegation of experts to negotiate with our people.   For this
discussion Mr. Hull has committees already organized in the
State Department, the Commerce Department, the Department
of Agriculture, and the Tariff Commission.   These men know a
great deal about trade conditions here and abroad.   All of these
committees are available to study the possibilities of expanding
trade with Iran to our mutual advantage.   But a special com-

mittee is likely to be constituted to bargain with the men from Iran. The Iranians will propose a list of things they would like to sell in this country more freely, and they will indicate some things they would be willing to import from the United States more liberally. We, of course, will give the Iranians two corresponding lists that we have made up. Then each side will study the effects of the imports into its country that have been proposed. On our side the effect of every proposed import will be studied and debated. Will it hurt our producers? If so, how much? Will the import benefit our consumers? How much? Will it be a good thing for the nation?

The process of bargaining may last for weeks or months, each side arguing its points in detail. The final result is, of course, a delicate balance of compromises. We have made concessions and so have they. It is a whole series of bargains, the net effect of which is to benefit both nations and to increase the trade between them. It is by no means a one-sided arrangement— just a means of admitting foreign goods into this country. On the contrary, the agreements have increased our exports far more than our imports. Secretary of Commerce Jesse Jones testified on April 13 that during the period 1934 to 1939 our imports from trade-agreement countries increased 22 per cent while our exports to the same countries increased 65 per cent. From the seller's point of view, then, we gained notably.

There is no evidence, either, that any of our home producers were seriously hurt. In some cases their profits have been reduced, but Mr. Hull's organization has been very gentle with all vested interests, well knowing that if they were seriously hurt the uproar in Congress would lead to the end of the trade-agreements program. It is true that the tariff adjustments made under these treaties have all been downward. It has been a way of carefully and gradually reducing our high tariff rates.

But what about the beneficiaries of our high tariffs? Do they have a chance to protest? At one stage of the process they do. Public notice is given and they can appear before a committee and present their arguments, though their lobbyists cannot influence the trade-agreements committees so much as they could a committee of Congress.

How does this new method of tariff making compare with the old method, whereby Congress tried in one big law to fix thousands of tariff rates at exactly the right points? The last congressional revision of the tariff took place in 1930. Hearings before the House Ways and Means Committee began January 7, 1929, and the crush of those desiring protection was so great that the hearings resembled a bargain counter. Schedules were made out covering weeks in advance, yet the schedule was always falling behind. Day after day the petitioners filed by, exhorted constantly to be brief in presenting their demands. The pressure was so great that five minutes was an age to the committee. Minutes were doled out by the chairman. Some petitioners were lucky to get three minutes—two minutes. At one time a crisis arose because only 118 witnesses had been heard in four days, whereas 184 were scheduled to appear. The witnesses had to be driven through faster and faster. The bankruptcy of the proceedings was openly confessed by cutting off witnesses who had more to say and were struggling to say it.

Representatives of important industries had perforce to be given more time, but all were urged to leave the rates they wanted in writing, and finally the committee attempted to digest the vast mass of written requests for higher tariffs presented to it. There was no attempt to check briefs, to require proof of the need for protection, or to secure the evidence of persons able to verify disputed testimony.

The contrast is evident between that kind of procedure and the long, patient consideration given by the Hull committees to a small fraction of the total tariff structure. Actually, it is impossible for the 531 laymen elected to our Congress to know where tariff duties ought to be fixed on many thousands of different articles. A very few members may by long and hard study make themselves able to pass intelligently on some tariff rates, as Cordell Hull did while in Congress, but very few can or will undergo the long labor required to master tariff problems.

Nor is it possible to give the laymen in Congress any tariff yardstick whereby they could legislate for the benefit of the nation. The formula most often proposed is "cost of production plus a reasonable profit," but consider where this leads. What is the cost of production of typewriters in this country? What is it abroad? How are we to find out? At one time we actually tried to get access to the records of foreign manufacturers. Many factors enter into cost of production and these factors often change rapidly, so that by the "cost of production" theory the tariff rate will be often obsolete by the time it is fixed. What also is a fair profit—for our producers and for theirs? Obviously all congressmen can do in trying to answer all these questions for thousands of rates is, in general, to vote the rates up or down.

By comparison, the Hull method is deliberate, careful, and continuous. It enables men with great knowledge of trade conditions to weigh the evidence for each proposed change. It is slow, but it operates continuously, there is never a sudden upheaval which unsettles the whole business structure of the nation.

It seems obvious that the business of tariff making has become far too complicated for any parliament to handle, but one final and dangerous objection is made to the Hull method. It is said that the trade agreements are really treaties and that they should be approved by a two-thirds vote of the Senate. At first glance this is reasonable, but in practice it would certainly mean the death of the trade-agreements program, for then the old practice of logrolling would hit the trade agreements with redoubled force, especially since a third of the senators could defeat any trade agreement, whereas a majority would be required to defeat a tariff law.

When the Congress made tariffs there was never much trouble in assembling a majority of the Senate, each senator getting his special tariff favors. The same custom would enable every economic interest in the country which thought it might be adversely affected by a trade agreement with Iran to enlist senators in opposition. Any requirement that the trade agreements be approved by two-thirds of the Senate would mean the end of the program.

With the world in chaos and likely to be for a long time, this is surely not the time to give notice to the world that we propose to revert to economic war—the precursor of shooting war. We are not required to play Santa Claus to the world, but we are compelled to live in it, to buy as well as sell, to trade with all the earth and to permit it to trade with us, to live and let live.

All of these axiomatic truths would be denied by a failure to continue the trade-agreements program. To kill it now would also give a death blow to all our hopes of organizing the United Nations into a shield and protection for our future against the colossal wastes and sufferings of global wars.

Notice how systematically the speaker sustains his leading idea. He answers questions in this order:

Why do you bring up this tiresome subject?

Why bother with it now?

Well, if I have to listen, how do they work out these trade agreements?

Aren't we losing business by lowering the tariffs?

You mean to say that no producer is hurt?

Why can't Congress make tariff as heretofore?

Aren't you just asking us to hand over more power to irresponsible bureaucrats?

Aren't we giving away too much already?

This needs more looking into. Suppose we let the agreements lapse and consider them after the war when things will all be different?

These are the questions that a thoughtful listener might ask. He might like more evidence from our own farmers, manufacturers, and cattle raisers as to the results of these trade agreements in the last 9 years. He might like to hear certain members of Congress, if there is as much opposition in Congress as Dr. Fleming implies. He would certainly appreciate hearing about a list of articles that he can buy cheaper now than he could before these trade agreements went into effect.

But if time is of the essence anywhere, it must be on the radio. The speaker can't give you everything in his strictly allotted time, and that is why he must be more mindful in selecting and condensing. Fortunately, it isn't necessary to satisfy everybody, and nobody asks for complete proof or demonstration. The thing would get too exhausting.

Dr. Fleming made two or three good points with enough illustrations and concrete statements of each proposition. He began his talk by showing an immediate need, and a danger to the listener (an appeal to fear—always a powerful motive). He continued with a brief explanation of the negotiations for trade agreements, gave proof of favorable results, compared the new scientific method with the old haphazard favoritism, warned of a widespread but specious and dangerous objection to negotiated agreements, and closed with a note of urgency, and of disaster if the trade-agreements program is discontinued.

We should speak of one other matter before we close this chapter. If the talk is given a title, that title should have something to hold the reader or listener. Can you think of something better, for instance, than "Shall the Hull Method of Tariff Making Be Ended?" It is appropriate and accurate enough but it doesn't sound exciting—and over the air *Hull* might be mistaken as a careless pronunciation of *whole*. The title also suggests the faintly disagreeable atmosphere of college debating. As an exercise and a reminder to study your own titles, try to improve it.

The title should have punch but it shouldn't be so breezy or bossy or jazzy as to suggest bluff or bad manners. Are any of the following titles better than Dr. Fleming's? Which are worse?

"Save the International Trade Agreements."

"Hull or Hell?"

"Will June 12 See the Death Blow to Peace Plans?"

"Better Business, Lower Prices."

"What Price Protection?"

"Will Congress Kill Our Foreign Trade?"

"Who Said Competition?"

"Does Business Want Free Enterprise?"

"The Tariff Racket."

The title should arouse curiosity and it should not give the show away. Such titles as "The Problems of Peace," "The Ladder of Success," "Paying for the War," "Your Duty As a Citizen" are dull. You turn from them instinctively and feel that the speaker will be ponderous and full of platitudes.

You know many of the titles that have sold books and speeches: *Acres of Diamonds, The Man Nobody Knows, It Can't Happen Here, Gone with the Wind, Death Takes a Holiday, The Fifth Freedom, Whither Midst Falling Due, The Lights Are Going Out.*

Your everlasting problem is to choose between the lively and the lifeless. The fundamental subjects of life are all commonplace enough, in the sense that everybody has a certain familiarity with them. You will try to galvanize them with a fresh and stimulating approach. Don't neglect the advertising in the headline.

CHAPTER V

Making Contact

You have organized your material, let us say, but have not yet begun to write your speech. Go back to the thought of showmanship for a moment and ask yourself whether you have made a genuinely vital contact with your audience. Your purpose and plan may be fundamentally sound, but you may still lack the proper bait or hook.

What do audiences "feed on" with relish? Well, they like best something about themselves and their children, something about their personal hopes and fears.

Self-preservation, we are told, ranks first among the impelling motives that prompt us to listen or to act. We are sensitive to anything that touches us or our families. The insurance agent first scares the father with the prospect of dying and leaving his wife and children penniless and in want. Motives of loyalty and self-respect are also involved in this situation. The motive of self-preservation operates in many directions. When the insurance man can't move his "prospect" through fear, he gets him through hope— shows him how he can build up an estate for the education of his children and an annuity for his old age.

Hope is just another aspect of fear. Almost everybody is conscious of the fear of death and the fear of want. "We have nothing to fear except fear," said President Roosevelt. Government propaganda intended to get total and efficient effort in war is mostly an appeal to fear. It is fear that makes us act.

So "you may view with alarm" and get results. The trouble is that so many politicians have cried "Wolf!" to get attention that your listeners may be a bit callous about matters that should be of deep concern. But the fear of God, of death, of taxes, of loss of health and job, is still a vital nerve that isn't hard to reach.

If your subject has nothing to frighten folks into listening, you may appeal to another motive that is almost as powerful. People crave attention, recognition, success, praise. The factory worker wants to be a foreman, the office worker a vice-president. All of us like to feel that we belong and amount to something. We want at least self-respect and the respect of others. The last despair is to admit irredeemable failure.

The pride, or vanity, of the ego takes many forms. The country weekly prospers because it mentions almost everybody in the community. Some people spend half their lives trying to get a little publicity. Others want to show off a car or a new home. If you can show your listeners how to get ahead or if you can demonstrate that they might be a lot worse off, you'll get attention.

We pick up a magazine and are suddenly impressed by the fact that three quarters of the ads have to do with sex appeal. They tell us to look better and smell better if we want to catch a man or a woman. Anything that will make us more attractive to the opposite sex can be made interesting to a large audience.

The lower, selfish, motives may be more fundamental but man has been conditioned to much higher motives. Young people want to give themselves to a worthy cause, they want to become part of a crusade. They will work and fight for the generous ideal. They will give their lives in sacrifice and struggle for the common good rather than disintegrate in the aimless round of meaningless routine. There is such a thing as inspiration, and many lives have been changed by the words of a speaker or the pages of a book. You can appeal successfully to the motives of courage, loyalty, sympathy, tolerance, fair play. You can get people to join a party or a society that demands hard or even dangerous work in a cause that stirs the imagination.

Love of country is patriotism mostly glorified in war. Battle is the greatest game of all, and many a dull and obscure civilian turns out to be a soldier-hero. He met the most significant challenge with everything in him and disclosed a spirit he himself had never suspected.

War—destruction and death between nations—we want to end forever, but there is an everlasting war between good and evil, truth and falsehood, between enterprise and aimlessness, between courage and cowardice, between faith and doubt, between hope and despair, between intelligence and dullness, between action and inertia. The speaker who studies his audience can always get supporters— soldiers for the good—if he can touch off that fire of inner excitement.

Sounds as though you had to be eloquent. If you don't feel quite up to it, consider another fundamental appeal to audience interest—entertainment. It is easier to satisfy because so many things pass for entertainment. The word is misleading. *Escape* may be more accurate.

Few persons have strong purpose, drive, or inner resources. That is why many are quickly bored. If they can't drive their cars, play cards, or go to a movie, they don't know what to do with themselves. They welcome anything that promises a diversion from a somewhat empty existence. They wish to escape from themselves and take part in someone else's richer experience.

Fortunately, all persons are sometimes in the mood for entertainment, for something different from what may have been occupying them for a prolonged period. Entertainment is not merely comedy or jazz. It is anything that captures involuntary attention and converts it to sustained interest.

Now the qualities of interestingness are pretty well known and have been often discussed. The *unusual* is one. Ripley has made a fortune out of his "Believe It or Not" oddities. Even Ibsen's college professor, the husband of Hedda Gabler, had a characteristic phrase, "Fancy that!" for any bit of news or circumstance that was not part of his ordinary daily experience. It may be a trivial matter. But think of the derivation of *trivial*. It comes from the Latin *trivium*, a place where three roads meet, a crossroad, the place where travelers met and exchanged gossip and news before newspapers existed. Their talk was mostly small stuff, later called trivial to mark the spot, but it was still of great interest to the listeners and still is. There are thousands of unusual pieces of fact and information lying around in science, psychology, art, biography, and literature to fascinate people. Today, almost anyone can give a lively talk on recent scientific discoveries that will increase everyone's comfort and income.

For the most powerful appeals to interest we must again go back to drama. Drama not only simulates life but concentrates attention more than any other form of composition. Its characteristic device is *conflict*, conflict between individuals, between groups, between ideas. Life itself is just a conflict, a perpetual struggle to overcome obstacles between us and what we want. When we relax from our own conflicts we go to see other battles—baseball, football, hockey, or a movie. Perhaps we read a book and are satisfied with a clash of opinion.

Every well-known political speech from Demosthenes to Roosevelt or Churchill has plenty of challenge and fight. Your own mild talk of explanation may seem to have little opportunity for conflict, but you may still be able to challenge common error in regard to your subject, or challenge the indifference the public may have revealed concerning it.

Dr. José Arce, distinguished Argentine surgeon and president of the Pan-American Medical Association, began his radio talk of October 24, 1942, with a challenge to common misconceptions about his country. He said:

While it is true that there is no lack of Americans who write about us after having visited Argentina and presumably studied us, it is also true that we, the Latins, encounter some difficulty in trying to understand the Anglo-Saxons. The Anglo-Saxons, however cultured and intelligent, are not always the best suited to perceive with accuracy the characteristics of Latin peoples, and especially the Spanish peoples.

It happens at times that our visitors let themselves be influenced by those who talk most, who are not always those who know most, or by information gathered from the people nearest at hand, who, again, are not always the best informed.

In Latin nations, those who hold public office have not always an accurate notion of the way the majority of the population feels. This results in wrong reports which we read from time to time, in the English language, about my country. Some of my compatriots then become angry and reply with notorious falsehoods about the English-language peoples, chiefly the United States of America.

As far as I am concerned, I neither become angry nor laugh, even when I see that our national hero, San Martin, is described as an adventurer. I simply regret in that case the ignorance of whoever wrote it, or the unfortunate circumstance that made him seek information from a poor source.

I come from Argentina, where the feelings of 90 per cent of the population are for the United Nations. I bring from the School of Medicine of the University, to which I belong, many messages written and signed by many of its professors, expressing to their colleagues in at least fifteen American universities, their sympathy and their solidarity in these moments of anxiety for this nation.

A third important factor of interest is *animation*, or *action*. Most plays and stories have plenty of movement, the stir of life. Still pictures do not attract like moving pictures. Give your descriptions a candid-camera quality that suggests that you have captured something spontaneous and alive. Use verbs of action. Cut out the pale and delaying adjectives. "Washington in Wartime" doesn't sound exciting. If it's politics, you expect a dull rehash; if it's description of buildings and departments, you are sure it's lifeless. Yet see how much animation and variety Eric Sevareid packs in these few paragraphs from a short broadcast on December 7, 1942.

Your capital city has changed in the interval between the two December 7's. There is a patch of darkness where the Capitol dome used to glow like a ball of white light in the evening. You will see a pin point of red light guiding the airplanes around the tip of the Washington Monument. The silver passenger planes land now with their window curtains drawn, and come to berths beside brown bombers and fighters. Soldiers shiver in the wind beside their antiaircraft guns on top of the government buildings. There are signs with a big "S" on the doorways telling you where to go for shelter in the air raid which has never come. On the dashboard of taxicabs you see small blocks of wood. They were meant to hold stretchers for the wounded. Now they are used for ash trays. Many cars have disappeared, but the traffic system remains the most bewildering in the world. Two days ago a streetcar got lost.

Soldiers and sailors from a half-dozen camps drift hopefully through the streets of a town which has an overabundance of women. In the White House, they can hear the music from the Stage Door Canteen on Lafayette Square. The deaths in traffic accidents have gone up, and juvenile delinquency has increased 40 per cent. Union Railroad Station is a great swarming junction for military trains from both north and south. Other trains bring hopeful civil service workers and still others haul away disappointed stenographers who could not face the cost of living nor the loneliness of the crowd.

Washington has not lost its perpetual look of being unfinished. A new gray city of offices rises across the Potomac. In the park of a famous private estate, identical rows of brick dormitories go up to house the army of women clerks. It is fashionable to live in a cramped Georgetown house, damp in winter, insufferable in summer. To be fashionable, men pay $300 a month rent, and live next door to Negroes who pay $50. Encroaching of the wealthy white has forced out the impoverished black.

Wealthy captains and colonels, with office commands, lunch in the Carlton Hotel, where a dish of ice cream is 65 cents. A year ago, they thought themselves lucky to get a safe job; now, they feel frustrated and they long for action. The State Department men still walk the block from their musty offices to the mustier Metropolitan Club, where the Scotch is still old and good. The crowd at the Press Club bar is a little deeper; by extreme exertions, the Press Club preserved tradition and avoided having to hire waitresses instead of waiters.

All manner of men come now to Washington. On the flag pole of the old Blair House, where Lee was offered command of the Union Armies, you see the bright standard of Poland or Ecuador or Peru. You see an Austrian archduke get on a crowded bus, and you chat with a former premier of France under the neon lights of a Hamburger Heaven.

Mr. Sevareid also illustrates, in the quotation above, another fundamental factor of interest—the *specific*, or the *concrete*. Many writers and speakers are content to amble along with dim generalities because they are too lazy to search for the illuminating example or details. Mr. Sevareid begins with, "Your capital city has changed." We instantly reply, "How?"

He might have continued with a summary of the difficulties about transportation, food, rent, and discomfort. Instead, he gives us at once a generous list of "for instances," with vivid, moving details—planes, streetcars, taxis, Stage Door Canteen, $300 rents, ice cream at 65 cents a dish, the Press Club bar, an archduke on a bus, a former premier of France under the neon lights of a Hamburger Heaven.

James Lawrence Fly, Chairman, Federal Communications Commission, has this paragraph in a speech delivered January 28, 1943. Notice how he goes at once from the general to the specific:

The research problems which radio engineers must conquer today would have baffled any scientist a generation ago. We need microphones, for example, which will transmit the human voice but not the engine noises of a four-motored bomber hurtling through the air at high speeds. We need direction-finding apparatus which will locate the plane, ship, or land station from which a given radio signal emanates. We need walkie-talkie radios, light enough to be carried into battle. Even the common variety of radio receiver must be re-engineered if it is to be used on board ship, in order to prevent telltale radiations from revealing the location of the ship to enemy raiders. Above all, we need absolute dependability in all war communications apparatus. Such design problems as these are daily being met and solved.

The specific and the concrete remind us that we must speak in terms and experiences that are *familiar*. The psychologist says that we must proceed from the known to the unknown. Nothing utterly new will interest us more than a moment unless it is somehow related to something familiar. "It's like this," says the teacher, as he holds the student's attention to a strange proposition by the method of comparison and contrast.

President Roosevelt has sometimes been accused of over-simplifying, of spending too much time in reducing the issues and abstractions of statecraft to obvious and familiar patterns of words and illustrations. But that has been the very secret of his immense success on the radio. "Fireside chats" sums up the President's method and art. You may recall this sample of his style:

First of all, let me state the simple fact that when you deposit money in a bank the bank does not put the money into a safe deposit vault.

It invests your money in many different forms of credit—bonds, commercial paper, mortgages, and many other kinds of loans. In other words, the bank puts your money to work to keep the wheels of industry and of agriculture turning around. A comparatively small part of the money you put into the bank is kept in currency —an amount which in normal times is wholly sufficient to cover the cash needs of the average citizen. In other words, the total amount of all the currency in the country is only a small fraction of the total deposits in all of the banks.

What, then, happened during the last few days of February and the first few days of March? Because of undermined confidence on the part of the public, there was a general rush by a large portion of our population to turn bank deposits into currency or gold—a rush so great that the soundest banks could not get enough currency to meet the demand. The reason for this was that on the spur of the moment it was, of course, impossible to sell perfectly sound assets of a bank and convert them into cash except at panic prices far below their real value.

On March 15, 1937, Fred A. Hartley, Jr., Congressman from New Jersey, gave a radio talk through the facilities of the National Broadcasting Company on taxes. Compared with our present war taxes the things Mr. Hartley spoke of now seem trivial, but notice how skillfully and concisely he combined the you-attitude, the profit motive, the unusual, the concrete, and the familiar to hold attention on a "dull" subject.

WHAT HIDDEN HAND TAKES YOUR MONEY?

This talk concerns your pocketbook. It is my purpose to present certain facts about the biggest bill you have to pay. That is your tax bill.

I can visualize those of my listeners who pay no income tax or real-estate tax saying, "Oh, let's tune in another program; this talk is of no interest to us."

On the contrary, I hope to prove that when we talk about tax-payers, no one is excepted. You pay more for taxes than you do for food or rent and twice as much as you spend for clothing. Yes, that's true, whether you pay an income tax and a real-estate tax or not. The earnings of three full months of your year's work or about 25 cents on every dollar you earn is what you pay to be governed.

There was a time when most of our revenue for government was raised by the direct income tax, which our people understood because they could see it and feel it. But today our taxes are sugar-coated and hidden in various business transactions, leaving most of us unconscious of the assessment. The trend in taxation has been based, apparently, on the theory that "where ignorance is bliss, 'tis folly to be wise." Taxation has become the art of so picking the goose as to secure the greatest amount of feathers with the least amount of squawking.

During the years I have served in Congress, I have seen several sales-tax bills defeated on the ground that such a tax would be unfair to the masses in the lower income brackets. And yet today we have such a tax on almost everything we buy, necessities as well as luxuries, the only difference being that it is a hidden tax and hardly one in a thousand realizes he's paid it.

Let's take a look at some of those taxes. You get out of bed in the morning from between sheets taxed at 4 cents a pound. You go into the bathroom and turn on the electric light taxed at 3 per cent of your bill. You brush your teeth with a dentifrice taxed at 5 per cent. The soap you used had a 5 per cent tax on it.

Then you dress. On your hosiery, shirt, shoes, and clothes you paid a tax of approximately 20 per cent. For example, there are sixty-three taxes on a suit of clothes, so that on a $35 suit there is a tax of $6.86.

You sit down to eat, and once again the tax collector is an uninvited guest. There are fifty-eight taxes on bread, thirty-eight taxes on meat, thirty-two taxes on canned food, forty-five taxes on sugar, 1½ cents on a quart of milk, or a tax assessment of over 20 per cent of the cost of all the food you eat. Your silverware, linens, dishes, and other household appliances each have the mark of the invisible tax collector. This sort of hidden taxation extends to almost every activity of your normal daily life.

You drive your car to work, and I'm wondering if, as a car owner, you realize that you are taxed 345 times. Yes, there are 27 taxes on the purchase of a car, 117 taxes on its upkeep, and 201 taxes on the oil and gas you use. The tax on gas is greater than its wholesale cost.

There are 146 taxes on drugs and medicines, amounting to one-third of their cost. Your insurance premium is taxed at from 15 to 20 per cent. If you hunt or fish, your gun and your rod bear a 2 per cent tax. Nor is your wife immune from such taxes. Her cosmetics, perfumes, furs, and jewels—if she is fortunate enough to possess them—are all taxed 10 per cent.

When you get home at night and sit down to a friendly rubber of contract, you have paid a 10 per cent tax on the cards you use. Other examples and the manner in which the tax is passed on to you could be related ad infinitum.

These taxes, which everyone is paying, may be startling. But they will fade into insignificance as compared with inevitable future taxes unless we give our attention to the solution of this perplexing problem.

Under the head of entertainment, you know what type of writing or speaking is most popular. It is narration, storytelling, and that is largely because of the element of *suspense*. You wouldn't read a detective story if it was prefaced by a paragraph or two summarizing the plot. You don't want to know how the story ends until you've had the pleasure of suspense, of guessing what's coming and of speculating on "who done it."

A speech that gives the story away in the opening remarks loses at once the factor of suspense. This is a serious matter, especially if the topic seems technical or in any other way forbidding. A playful beginning, a short anecdote, and a step-by-step treatment that has surprise, create an atmosphere of excitement and keep the listener in a state of pleasurable anticipation. To do this without letting the embroidery distract from the central pattern requires restraint and a sense of balance. Here are two opening passages that will illustrate what we mean:

There was a king, once upon a time, who was very fond of clothes. He had a robe for every hour of the day. The people of his kingdom were always seeking new silks and new styles and new colors for him, until one day two strange men came to the palace and said they could weave the finest fabric anyone could imagine. But theirs would not be ordinary cloth, they said; theirs would be a magic cloth. If a *stupid* man looked at it he would not be able to see it at all, it would be invisible to him. If a king's courtier was *unfit* for his office, and looked at this cloth, it would become invisible to him. "Ah!" said the king, "that is just what I want; make me robes of that magic cloth and then I

shall see which of my officials are unfit and I shall know a dunce
when I see one."

W. J. CAMERON.

Here is a sloping cellar door. Take a watering can and sprinkle
a quart of water at its top. Measure the amount which slides
off. Except for a little evaporation, the whole quart will be at
the bottom almost instantly. Now tack a piece of thick carpet on
the door. Again pour the quart of water on the carpet. Your
measuring trough at the bottom will be lucky if it receives the
merest trickle at first. Observe that the trickle continues for a
long time.

This is the story of water erosion in its simplest form. The
cellar door is any land with a slope; the canful of water is rainfall; the bare boards are bare-plowed fields; the carpet is a natural
cover, either grass or forest. In the first case most of the water
comes down, dissolving the rich topsoil and taking it along. In
the second case, the cover absorbs the water, puts much of it into
ground storage to be slowly released over periods of scanty rainfall.
Almost no soil comes down.

STUART CHASE.

Dialogue is the essence of drama and storytelling and can
often be used very easily by the speaker. Instead of making
all your points by comparatively heavy explanation convert
one or two of them into the more sprightly form of give and
take. Note this good example from a speech made before
the war by Raymond Gram Swing:

A few years ago a Russian friend of mine went over to Paris and
there visited Miliukoff, one of the leaders of the Russian Duma
during its brief and frustrated life. Miliukoff told him that he
just had a visit from a Communist from Russia, a young man who
had all his education from the Soviet state. This young man
asked him some questions.

"Is it a fact, as I have been told," he asked, "that in the old
Russia there were many political parties and they all disagreed?"

"Yes," said Miliukoff, "there were many parties and they all disagreed."

"And is it a fact," asked the young Communist, "that there were many newspapers and magazines that also had different theories about public affairs?"

"Yes," said Miliukoff, "there were thousands of newspapers and periodicals, and most of them disagreed, too."

"How odd!" exclaimed the young Communist, "when there is only one truth."

That young Russian, it seems to me, gives us in a nutshell the best there is to say for the controlled press. If there is only one truth, what could be more intelligent and justifiable than to suppress lies? What could be wiser than to see to it that the printing presses turn out simply the one truth? I must say that I have moments when I envy the young man from Russia and wish I might have, shall I say, a holiday, during which I believed that there is only one truth, and that I was in possession of it.

Here is part of a fine speech delivered by R. W. Jepson several years ago, over the British Broadcasting System. He has been speaking about people "whose political views are limited to a set of simple and easily remembered catchwords and slogans." He illustrates the types with dialogue like this:

Have you ever come across the man who buttonholes you and poses you with a question and insists on your answering, "Yes" or "No"? He will say to you, "Now then, are you a Free-trader, or aren't you?" And you might reply, "Well, the removal of all restrictions and barriers on international trade would be an ideal thing to my mind. But as things are . . . ." Then he will burst in and say, "Come along now, I asked you a plain question. Give me a plain answer." Once again you will probably stammer out a few "buts." Then he will tell you you are hedging. "Either you are, or you aren't," he will say. "Which is it? 'Yes' or 'No'?" You know the kind of person: the real whole-hogger.

Then there's the sort of man who will put you down as an extremist on the slightest pretext. If you express the slightest sympathy with one aim of a political party, he will credit you with all the views of that party in their extreme form. For instance, you might show some slight misgiving about the possible effects of the recent law on sedition. You might say you were a bit doubtful about its effect on freedom of speech. Then he would say, "Oh! I've no patience with you. You're an out-and-out Communist." (And, by the way, he is pretty vague if you ask him what he means by some of the labels he is so fond of using.) Again, if you ventured to suggest that our parliamentary procedure was a bit slow and cumbersome he would say, "Oh, you want to do away with it altogether. Wouldn't you prefer a dictatorship?"

Every word is a *symbol* of something in the mind. Print stands for sound, and everything seems to stand for something else—the lion for courage, the oak for strength, the rabbit for timidity, the tiger for ferocity, the donkey for the Democratic party, the elephant for the Republican party, the bulldog for Yale, the terrier for Boston University, and so on.

Every cartoon grows out of our habit of symbolizing. Like the caricature, the symbol expresses at least one point of obvious resemblance, though in other respects there may be distortion or misleading suggestion. Notice these stereotyped labels—*Uncle Sam*, *John Bull*, *bloated plutocrat*, *horny-handed labor*, *hidebound Republican*, *starry-eyed New Dealer*. We use the symbol for praising or condemning. It's easier to put a tag on somebody than to go through the difficult business of analyzing and reasoning. Samuel Crowther began a magazine article entitled "Slaves to the Slogan— Catch Words as Collars," with this paragraph:

"You take the arguments, take all the right and justice in a political campaign," said a shrewd and seasoned politician to me

the other day, "and if I can get a catchword or a slogan, I don't
need any right or justice to make a good run against you and
maybe to beat you.   Even if I don't get a slogan for my man but I
do get a first-class epithet for yours, I will rustle you then, too."

Name calling suggests spite or fight but everything has
to have a name. The public welcomes a name to give
some expression to its inarticulate and confused notions
about complicated issues and personalities.   Indeed, who
doesn't want a crystallizing phrase?   Even the intellectuals
still use some pretty musty catchalls like *reactionary*, *progressive, wishful thinking, inferiority complex, ideology.*

Wendell Willkie put the significance of all this very neatly
in the opening paragraphs of his Lincoln Day speech in
1940:

A stencil is a useful tool for painting letters and words on a sign.
No matter how often you use it, the letters always stay the same
and the sign always says the same thing.   And it is a great human
temptation to use a stencil as much as possible, not only for painting signs—but also for thinking.

Now in the course of the last decade there has been developed
a set of what you might call political stencils for the Republican
party.   And some of these stencils have not been very flattering.
I will confess that we ourselves have manufactured a number of
them.   But our opponents, the Democrats, have always been
glad to get others made for us and to pass them around—free of
charge.

It is customary, in painting this sign, to use black paint.   The
sign usually describes a Republican as a socially unconscious
hidebound conservative, or even a reactionary.   It says that he is
a narrow, unknowing nationalist and that the end of the world
will come if he is elected to power.

It's a good thing that we can laugh at these misconceptions.
But just the same, my fellow Republicans, it is time to put an

end to them. It is time to sweep up all the old stencils and dump them on the scrap heap.

The *analogy* is a story that has symbolic purpose. It, too, makes clear a somewhat similar situation now faced by a speaker or being discussed by him. Almost every story, serious or humorous, available for public speaking must be an analogy, must have this quality of relevant comparison or contrast. It must refer to the subject of the talk in some illuminating way. Here, in the opening paragraph of Sir J. Arthur Thomson's article in *The Atlantic Monthly* of June, 1930, is a fine example of this relevant use:

The loggerhead turtle lays its eggs on a sandy shore, and when the young ones are hatched out they dig their way to the surface and make for the sea. By careful experiments Prof. G. H. Parker of Harvard has shown that the young loggerheads are not guided by hearing or smelling the sea, nor do its waters in the strict sense come within their vision. But the loggerheads have an inborn bias to make for the more illumined horizon. If an upward slope is artificially arranged, they will creep uphill if it is toward the opener light; if a barrier like a fence is arranged so that the more illumined horizon is inland, then inland they will go. On the floor of a tub the little creatures crawl about at random, for the prospect is equally dull all around; but if the tub is inverted and the adventurers are placed on the platform, they will make unerringly in the right direction and topple over toward the sea! Comparing great things to little, we may liken man to these loggerheads; he has, on the whole, a bias for making toward the more illumined horizon. The question we wish to ask is, *What new prospects are before us?*

Effective analogies are often discovered in the lives of our forebears, in their quoted remarks that seem so strikingly appropriate today. Of course, the incidents and the quotations should not be so familiar as George Washington crossing the Delaware or Lincoln's Gettysburg address. The cherry tree, Lincoln's shovel, Patrick Henry's "Give me liberty or give me death!" are played out. Every speaker should become sophisticated enough to recognize the hackneyed, worn-out story and quotation that people are simply sick of. Listeners still love the old heroes and shrines and never tire of hearing of them so long as there is a touch of novelty in the reference.

Rev. Walton E. Cole shows how to get immediate response by his skillful use of this device in a Church of the Air broadcast, February 7, 1943:

Some months ago I was the guest preacher for the oldest congregation in New England. As I stood in that pulpit in Plymouth, Mass., I noticed in the announcement calendar a picture of their first church building, erected by the Pilgrims in 1621. That simple log structure was a combination fortress and meeting-house. Two cannons were mounted on the roof while provision was made on the ground floor for the worship of God.

I reflected that after more than three centuries we were once more mounting cannons on the roof of the citadel of America. Would we exhibit the realistic courage which sustained these creative pioneers of the American tradition?

The courageous spirit of the Pilgrims is gloriously recorded in William Bradford's *History of Plymouth Plantation*. Bradford tells us that when the idea of a journey to the New World was first announced it "raised many variable opinions . . . and caused many fears and doubts . . . it was a great design and subject to many unconceivable perils and dangers." And then came the reply which is one of the noblest passages in the heritage of America. Here are words that sound a bugle to our era, words that stiffen our backbone, words that strengthen our morale:

"It was answered that all great and honorable actions are accompanied with great difficulties, and must be both enterprised and overcome with answerable courages. It was granted that the dangers were great but not desperate; the difficulties were many but not invincible."

You and I confront our own dangers and difficulties. Where shall we discover and how shall we maintain answerable courages?

The humorous story, for the speaker's purpose, should also be an analogy, should present an idea or a situation that has something in common, something for relevant comparison and contrast, with the topic of discussion. Not even the professional comedian would think of reciting a collection of unrelated "funny" stories. He says, "Last week I was visiting my brother and was surprised to find," etc., or "When I got back to the hotel last night," or "This gasoline business is getting worse and worse. Over on L— Street a filling station has a new sign . . . ."

He tries to connect his patter with the experience of his listeners, to make his fiction sound real and actual, to give it the quality of the life and atmosphere about him. When Bob Hope toured the Army and Navy camps he repeated favorite gags frequently, but he always tried to make them grow naturally out of his experience in the particular camp he happened to be visiting.

Here is an example of the humorous analogy, used by Maurice Samuels to begin a serious talk:

There is a story told about a professor who was discussing with his colleagues the manner in which the subject of love had been treated in a recent novel, when someone interrupted him with the question, "Professor, have you ever been in love?" The professor stopped short, answered "No!" and withdrew from the gathering. Several months later he returned to a similar meeting with the announcement, "Gentlemen, let us begin the discussion all over again: I have remedied the defect!" I used to think that story clever, but its point has disappeared for me, now that, having been to Palestine, I stand before you, and you ask me, "Well, what have you to say?" It seems to me now that the professor, after his adventure, if it was a true adventure, would have been much less prepared to discuss the subject than before; the deeper his emotions had been, the less able he would have been to give them form. And if the story goes to illustrate anything at all, it is the fact that the professor had been conducting an academic experiment; he was still a professor—and not a lover.

You see, the radio speaker, like every other speaker, must be more than logical; he must be psychological. He must "throw a line" that will firmly hook into the wants, the desires, even while he casts another into the reasoning, the detached, objective thinking of his audience. "Gain the heart," said Lord Chesterfield to his son, "or you gain nothing."

Let Woodrow Wilson sum up for Socrates, Caesar, Chesterfield, and the long line of leaders who learned how seldom mind prevails over ego. In a speech to the New York Southern Society he said:

We talk a great deal about being governed by the mind, by intellect, by intelligence, in this boastful day of ours; but as a matter of fact, I don't believe that one man out of a thousand is governed by his mind.

Men, no matter what their training, are governed by their passions, and the most we can hope to accomplish is to keep the handsomest passions in the majority.

CHAPTER VI
The Style of the Radio Talk

Eight-ninths of an iceberg is below water. Only one-ninth of its impressive bulk is apparent to the eye. All good writing and speaking is something like that. The mulling over, the growing, and and the planning take place in the hidden recesses of the mind. The actual writing may be only the last ninth of a long process of composition.

With all the facts and details before them in well-chosen order some writers dash off this last lap (it's a marathon now) with sure, swift confidence and precision. They just complete the sentences suggested in the outline and clarify and amplify the illustrations and instances briefly noted in the plan. The result may be satisfactory, too, because the purpose may be merely information for a group that desires, above everything else, clear, progressive argument or exposition.

But the writer for radio will often find this last lap the most difficult and discouraging of all. He has two problems and they are problems of style that may baffle the most experienced. First, he must write in the rhythms of talk; and second, he must find the words and phrases that are called magic, that cast the spell of attention on an audience which says, "Make it good, brother, or I'm on my way to a program I ought to be listening to, anyway." Now these rhythms and combinations of words are so simple that the untrained writer is constantly overlooking them. He bedevils his script with big words and fancy phrases. These

71

give him flat and foggy areas of wasteland instead of the picturesque, alluring country he thinks he is creating.

"Rhythms of talk" does not imply that you must altogether confine yourself to the meager, insipid, and monotonous patterns that often pass for talk. The business-letter writer is often advised to write as he talks. Yes, he should avoid such banalities as "Yours of the sixteenth received and contents noted. In compliance with your request, beg leave to state," etc. Nevertheless, his talk may not be much better because it is a long-winded rigmarole lacking in clearness, conciseness, and compulsion. He may be ignorant of the most obvious things about style. The model for the radio speaker should include the flexibility, ease, and vivacity of the best conversationalists.

The first thing you notice about good oral style is that the sentence structure is shorter, simpler, less complex than the average of printed or written style. This is natural because no speaker can improvise with the variety, ingenuity, delicacy, or subtlety of a man who sits at a desk and patiently writes and rewrites until he has made a sentence that fits harmoniously and beautifully into the mosaic that will be his finished composition. If he did, his listeners would say he sounded like a book. And, what is more important, they could not follow him easily enough to get pleasure out of his speech or to listen to the whole of it. It is one thing to read a book leisurely, going back over a sentence when it seems a bit obscure. It is something else to catch words out of the air and get their complete implications at once.

At any rate, your radio audience would hardly tolerate a passage like this:

Against this, as it appears to me, conclusive view of the sub-ject, it has been urged that this power is expressly conferred on the Supreme Court by that portion of the Constitution which provides that the judicial power shall extend to all cases in law and equity arising under the Constitution, the laws of the United States, and treaties made under their authority. I believe the assertion to be utterly destitute of any foundation. It obviously is the intention of the Constitution simply to make the judicial power commensurate with the law-making and treaty-making powers; and to vest it with the right of applying the Constitution, the laws, and the treaties, to the cases which might arise under them, and not to make it the judge of the Constitution, the laws, and the treaties themselves. In fact, the power of applying the laws to the facts of the case, and deciding upon such application, constitutes, in truth, the judicial power. The distinction between such power and that of judging the laws will be perfectly apparent when we advert to what is the acknowledged power of the court in reference to treaties or compacts between sovereigns.

That is only half of the paragraph, and it is a tribute to your powers of concentration if you followed it closely to the end. And yet this is a passage from one of America's great orators, John C. Calhoun. It is part of a speech delivered in the Senate in 1833. It took Calhoun two days to give his whole argument against the force used by the administration of President Jackson on the state of South Carolina. It is a masterpiece of logic but it undoubtedly put most of the senators to sleep or drove them out of the chamber.

Calhoun was an intellectual giant but his language was too formal and severe even for his own day. His legal and technical terminology, his precise exposition in abstract formulas, had not enough concreteness, color, and warmth to suit popular audiences. He lacked the impressive showmanship of Webster or the fiery exuberance and personal magnetism of Henry Clay.

Thurman Arnold, in an address to the Illinois State Bar Association, quoted this passage from Homer Lea's book, *The Valor of Ignorance:*

Whenever a nation becomes excessively opulent and arrogant, at the same time being without military power to defend its opulence or support its arrogance, it is in a dangerous position. Whenever the wealth and luxury of a nation stand in inverse ratio to its military strength, the hour of its desolation, if not at hand, approaches.   When the opulence and unmartial qualities of one nation stand in inverse ratio to the poverty and military prowess of another, while their expansion is convergent, then result those inevitable wars wherein the commercial nation collapses and departs from the activities of mankind forever.

Lea wrote his book 34 years ago and made an extraordinary analysis and prophecy of present world conditions. Other passages quoted by Arnold are clearer and much more specific. This one, however, though it contains striking phrases like "opulent and arrogant," and "the hour of its desolation, if not at hand, approaches," is still somewhat involved for speaking. The sentences are too long and contain dead spots like "inverse ratio" and "contingent" and "unmartial."

George Barton Cutten, president of Colgate University, used this same idea in his Commencement address of May 10, 1942, but presented it, if not in colloquial form, at least in the simpler rhythm and concreteness of talk. He said:

We can see written across the face of our civilization in words of blazing brightness, "Luxury and Comfort," and these, when translated, spell "Softness."   Softness has two disastrous effects— in the first place it makes us indisposed or unable to recognize danger, and in the second place, if continued sufficiently long, it renders us incapable of defending ourselves.   Comfort, with its glamour, its seduction, its attraction, and its insidious infiltration, is the fifth column of civilization. When our civilization gave us so many things others want, and when these luxuries and comforts cause us to be unprepared if not unable to defend ourselves, then war ensues, which threatens, if it does not destroy, our civilization.

Note the arresting force of such expressions as "written across the face," "luxury and comfort," "softness," "glamour," "seduction," "insidious infiltration," "fifth column of civilization."

Dr. Cutten is addressing an audience seated before him. Parts of his address are more oratorical than conversational. He illustrates the difficulty of addressing a crowd and a few listeners in the home at the same time. The radio audience must adjust itself to the mood and the situation of the visible audience. Examine for a moment two concluding paragraphs of Dr. Cutten's address:

If I were asked to name the twentieth century sin I would not hesitate a moment: it is dodging responsibility. This is the age of alibi. We not only like it, but we are trained for it. Where is the sturdy independence and unbridled initiative of our fathers? That was all antiquated foolishness. If they wanted the forests cleared, cabins built, crops planted, Indians conquered, mines developed, roads constructed, or rivers bridged they should have been aware of modern methods—they didn't know the A. B. C. of the twentieth century technique. If they had only had C.C.C., N.Y.A., W.P.A., how easy it would have been! And the very easiness would have been their downfall. Our nation would have died aborning. Thank God for their resoluteness; thank God for their hardihood; thank God for their courage; and thank God for their self-reliance. . . .

Take away the flaccid and flabby and give us men upon whom we can rely; take away the comfort seekers and give us burden bearers; take away the frail and the weak and restore the strong and efficient. Oh, God! take away our comforts and our ease and our enjoyment and our petty satisfaction, and give us tasks that are hard, assignments that are fatiguing, toil that is exacting, and drudgery that is wearying. We want to be men, prove us. Don't let this nation crumble.

Dr. Cutten doesn't sound like a New Deal Democrat. He stresses the old-fashioned virtues and the old-fashioned rugged individualism. He uses a bit of sarcasm to indicate his doubt about the quality of the modern generation and thanks God frequently for what he fears we have lost. He closes with a somewhat old-fashioned prayer and ends up with two short, sharp, vigorous sentences that tie up his message with a crisp finality.

The writer swings a mean pen. You sense in him the mission of Jeremiah and you enjoy his rhythmic, cadenced soaring into oratory. He likes the mouth-filling phrases: "age of alibi," "unbridled initiative," "the flaccid and flabby," "burden bearers," "toil that is exacting," "drudgery that is wearying." There is something stirring in all this, not to say eloquent, even though you suspect portions of it to have less sense than sound.

About two weeks after Pearl Harbor *The Nation* had an article by Jonathan Daniels, former editor of the *Raleigh News and Observer*. It was scarcely longer than an editorial and dealt with the same fears expressed by Dr. Cutten. It was an inspiring call to opportunity, however, rather than a solemn note of warning.

Notice its more familiar style. The newspaperman is more intimate and sounds more realistic. He seems to feel the pulse of the people more surely, and his quick appraising glance goes below the surface superficiality and reveals the healthy vitality and audacity that have always characterized America. He loves the pioneers but doesn't go reverent about them. They were good and tough, but the country is today full of men of the same stuff, and he shows you where to find them. Mr. Daniels, too, points out weaknesses but isn't discouraged by them. They are actually part of the terrific strength that is America. His talk is not a prayer for good men but a demand for action—and the response is "Let's go!"

We reprint the article here because of its style and because of its alert sense of audience attitude and doubt. The sentences are short, with an occasional longer one for variety. There are many details about places and people. Humor, shrewdness, insight give warmth and conviction. The writer avoids the usual highfalutin flourishes that depress us with their hints of quackery. This is good radio style, personal in its you-attitude, public in its ample dignity and force. It is eloquence without "oratory."

THE HOUR OF ELATION[1]

It is not hard to scare me. Say "Boo" and I'll jump. I don't like little unfamiliar noises in the dark. But it is going to take me a long time to be afraid about the essential strength and the essential security of America. Plenty of people have been scared in America. The first people who came to it were timid on a sea reputed to be full of monsters. The little people in the little boats who came slowly to fill its wilderness from one sea to another were frightened in the dark the big trees made and in the disturbing brightness which filled the prairies. They jumped and scurried. At Lexington and Concord the shots heard round the world began a six years' war. Bull Run was the Union's rout, from which Congressmen tumbled still running into Washington. But beyond terror, we have also and always been a people terrible in strength. We still are.

[1] *The Nation*, December 20, 1941. Reprinted by permission.

An American really doubtful today about the security of a republic which sprawls across a whole continent, full of half the riches of the world and the richest people of the world and the richest people in skills and strength on this earth, is not only a rabbit but a silly rabbit. There are some such native rabbits. Some have seen planes in empty skies. A good many of them poured stocks into a market of panic without once wondering where they would put the money they were paid except in the great, sound investment of America. Where is a dollar worth anything except in the destiny of America? Where on this earth is a life worth anything but in that destiny? When could there ever be a better time to be an American than in an hour when an American has the privilege to stand up to the full meaning of that word?

The sailors who manned the clipper ships are not gone. Our farms and cities are full of them. The craftsmen who turned the first wheels crowd the greatest industrial plant on earth. The fighting men did not die with our fathers. Our destiny did not play out when we began to play an arrogant game with dollars. The poor are not new, nor the slanders about them. The big, strong, restless, seeking poor move now as they have always moved. The country boys, the street boys, have never been truly caught in dead-end streets or on lanes which just petered out in the pasture. They moved with the destiny of America. Death is not new among us any more than the willingness to die has disappeared. There are hard hands, hard heads, hearts willing to be tough between our oceans, on ships upon them and on islands, in planes in the old, old sky. Lusty strong men and women, we are not a rabble but a race. The time has not gone in which we are willing to play with destiny for beers, or to fight in its name for a better world.

There never could have been a time when it was a greater privilege to be an American than now. The twenties are gone with self-indulgence. The thirties have disappeared with self-pity. The forties are here in which Americans stand on a continent as men—men again fighting in the crudest man terms—

for ourselves and also for that destination in decency for all men of which our settlement, our spreading, was always a symbol. In an America grown magnificently male again we have a chance to fight for a homeland with the full meaning of homeland as a world that is fit to be the home of man.

Fear at such a time? It is the hour for elation. Here is the time when a man can be what an American means, can fight for what America has always meant—an audacious, adventurous seeking for a decent earth. The gullies in our earth mark not only our waste but our labor. The slums in our cities are where we stumbled when our strongest folk in peacefulness sometimes grew fat. All the weak, bad things are only shadows beside our destiny now.

No people have done so much to light the dark places at home. Sometimes we seemed to build bridges and schoolhouses while other nations built ships and planes. Sometimes we seemed to think of the poor while others thought only of soldiers. That is not loss now. That emphasis in our peace is still the emphasis in our war. That aim at home is the basis of our strength in the world. The American dream for people is still what underlies the irresistible power of our arms. That American dream is a world force now, the force of men whose whole history has been a movement toward the chance of freedom, even if they had to seize it from the wilderness, subdue a continent to secure it. Aroused now, we can show a strength which will not only mean terrible war but the possibility of a splendid peace.

We are alive—rudely wakened. That is not basis for fear but sign that our destiny survives. We are men again in America.

You have already observed how Mr. Daniels gets emphasis and force out of small, plain, unpretentious words. Glancing through the article again for the things that make it interesting, we underline a few words and phrases— "scare," "boo," "timid," "little people in the little boats," "jumped and scurried," "beyond terror," "sprawls," "silly rabbit," "arrogant game," "the big, strong, restless, seeking poor," "just petered out in the pasture," "lusty," "not a rabble but a race," "play with destiny for beers," "magnificently male," "the hour for elation," "gullies," "slums where we stumbled," "men again in America."

The homely, vital words of everyday use are still the best for clear, sharp, bold, moving expression. That doesn't mean that you should not use polysyllabic words at all. Every word has its proper use, but inexperienced writers like the roll of longer words because they suggest more dignity and formal education. But if the words have little specific meaning for the listener, if they are mostly cold or vague abstractions, they are just duds that fail to explode in the hearts and minds of the audience.

The longest word Daniels uses is *magnificently*. Coupled with *male*, its impact is terrific. The rhythm, alliteration, and suggestion of the phrase are final, inevitable—just right. You linger to take in more of its world of implications and wish you had this knack of turning up the right word.

But we are straying from the point we started to make— that a word must be tested by what it will yield in the given situation. In one spot it may be barren, in another it may be fertile. Here it may be lifeless, there it may be electric.

The Anglo-Saxon monosyllables are not always the most appropriate. Indeed, there are none for certain common concepts. There are many words from the Latin, Greek, Arabic, and other languages that we should use and must use. *Government, parliamentary, constitutional, phonetic, antediluvian, heterogeneous, pandemonium, intramural, loquacious, hypercritical* are all good words, often the best for your specific needs. They are chiefly words of the mind and not of the heart.

One of the common temptations of the novice with the pen is the excessive use of glamorous words—*wonderful, dazzling, deathless, ravishing, intense, thrilling, enthralling*, etc. Advertisers have spoiled a lot of powerful stimulants by using them too often and too carelessly. The high-pressure stuff is extravagant with our reserves and defeats itself. All emphasis is no emphasis, and the skilled writer hesitates to use words that have had the juice squeezed out of them.

Eric Knight spoke of this on a CBS broadcast, July 19, 1942. He was discouraged with words. And yet he found the simple words adequate to give you the flashes he remembered—the bits of moving pictures. Common words don't get commonplace. They are of our flesh and blood. We can't live without them. It is the fancy words that lose their luster and make-up when we flirt with them too much.

Knight was a novelist, a man who knew that style makes all the difference. His short radio speech sounded so easy and effortless that you were liable to forget that conscious craftsmanship was necessary to give the style its casual and unstudied air. Well, see for yourself.

ONE REMEMBERS

Democracy, liberty, freedom, courage, fortitude—these are precious things. So precious, that perhaps we should ration the number of times a man may speak of them during his life—lest the ear become dulled to the names, and the things themselves lose their flaming, sharp-edged meaning.

One is aware of that today in speaking of Britain. The words have been used up.

And words would not make you really understand the shattered stones of Plymouth, Coventry, Liverpool, London, or Hull. Words alone can make no man understand the ungentle rain from heaven of bombs and screaming steel.

My mind does not want to seek words for these things—my mind does not even want to remember them.

As I look back, I find my mind wants to remember—what? Only about people—the common man and woman who, in total war, must suffer the war.

One remembers flashes—like bits of moving pictures—of people. The children—sitting in the schools, eating, and behind them, on the blackboard, the words: "Your eggs—come from Uncle Sam." Lend-lease food.

One remembers broken, funny incidents: The night the air raid sirens came howling up the Thames from the east like wolves in the hills, and an old maid from down the hall knocked on our door and asked to come in. She wore a dressing gown and curl papers and she was embarrassed. So we made tea—and she explained herself. She said, "It isn't that I mind dying, so much. But—they will always come as I'm in the bathtub and one doesn't want to die in—in an undignified way."

One remembers those things—incidents of common people: A sailor wearing a piece of mistletoe in his cap and whistling at a girl as he comes on leave at Christmas—the Anglican minister saying grace over one can of lend-lease meat in the rectory kitchen beside his seventh bombed-out church in the East End slums—the people sharing their sandwiches on trains which no longer have dining cars—the night shifts of the factories and the girls singing above the noise of the machines—singing the popular American songs that Bing Crosby sings.

For the people of Britain often sing, today. They sing aloud in the cities as they walk in the total blackout. You sing, because— well, for one thing, other people hear you and don't bump into you. And you sing because, somehow, the spirit is freer than it ever was before.

A style like that is developed by reading aloud what you write. You will soon discover by the way they sound whether your sentences are too long and complicated. Length is not a sure test because if the sentence is simple and loose, not holding too much emphasis in suspense through subordinate clauses, there will be no trouble following it. Notice the paragraph above beginning "One remembers those things." It is all one sentence technically, and it is almost a hundred words in length. If you followed literally the advice to keep sentences well within thirty words, you might lose some excellent effects.

Knight's one long sentence sounds like several short sentences, a series of afterthoughts flowing naturally out of "incidents of common people."

Look again at the sentence in the last paragraph of Knight's talk, "You sing, because—well, for one thing, other people hear you and don't bump into you." "You" is calculated and deliberate there, not an accident of spontaneous choice. And notice that broken effect, "because—well, for one thing," etc. Wouldn't that fool you? It sounds so natural and unpremeditated, as though the speaker were ad-libbing, without a script. We just succumb to a charm that has its method. Well, you're enrolled in the charm school now and should learn at least some of the easier devices for pleasing people.

CHAPTER VII

Reports to the Nation

After all this talk of showmanship and dramatizing, you may be discouraged by the feeling that what you have to offer just doesn't lend itself to that sort of supercharging. You are giving plain fare with little seasoning and no dessert. It is information and explanation that can't be dressed up and would sound silly if it were.

That is sensible comment, a sign of good taste, but it implies that you haven't yet trained your nose for news. Everybody, with a little thought and practice, can become a pretty good reporter, and he doesn't, like most reporters, have to make himself disagreeable in the process.

The newspaper reporter must learn to get vital and essential facts. He is constantly reminded that he must get the *who*, the *what*, the *where*, the *when*, the *how*, and the *why* of every event and situation that he reports. He is taught to discover the more interesting and significant of the issues involved and "play them up" for his readers. He is driven to get the "human-interest stories" behind the news, but he is also driven to acquire a shrewd, practical evaluation of information. He knows what is worth following up and how to get attention for the details likely to be of greatest interest to the public.

Sometimes the reporter has a problem much like yours. He's got to examine a solid piece of literary or political or scientific learning and write a short and interesting summary of its contents. He may not enjoy the assignment; he may, in fact, be greatly depressed at the prospect of plodding through hundreds of dull and difficult pages in search of he knows not what. He may even recall an anecdote told by a reporter of Civil War days. Anthony Gross, in *Lincoln's Own Stories*,[1] tells this one:

The President was once called upon in reference to a newly invented gun, concerning which a committee had been appointed to make a report.

The "report" was sent for, and when it came it was found to be of the most voluminous description. Mr. Lincoln glanced at it and said, "I should want a new lease of life to read this through!" Throwing it down upon the table, he added, "Why can't a committee of this kind occasionally exhibit a grain of common sense? If I send a man to buy a horse for me, I expect him to tell me his *points*—not how many *hairs* there are in his tail."

There is still plenty of room, especially in this age of research, for reports "of the most voluminous description," but we can sympathize with Lincoln's impatience. He wanted to know at once whether the gun had been thoroughly tested, whether it was practical, what it would cost, whether we had facilities to manufacture it in large quantities, and how long it would take; what, in short, it could contribute in winning the war. The report should have been prefaced, or followed, by a very brief summary of these pertinent "points."

Edward R. Murrow did a fine job in reporting the Beveridge report over the radio. He didn't just ramble through it vaguely, with misgiving. His trained mind suggested without effort the questions for which he wanted answers—and that is the test, as well, of the efficiency expert and the scientist. Creative ability is largely the

[1] Harper & Brothers, New York.

ability to discover the vital questions. When these are clearly posed, the answers are not long in arriving.

At any rate, Murrow knew the questions his audience wanted answered. He treated them in this order:

Who is Beveridge?

What's his report about?

What does he know about the subject?

Who asked him to put on such a big show?

Is he a Communist? an impractical professor? an aristocrat who doesn't really know anything about the poor?

What's he planning to insure us against?

How much would I have to pay in?

What would I get if I were out of work?

For how many weeks would I get it?

When could I retire and how much would I get?

Sounds pretty good, but do you think it will go through?

What are the politicians saying about it?

Any big business kicking?

How is the government going to pay for all this in addition to the war debts?

Mr. Murrow, chief of CBS foreign correspondents, gave this talk from London on December 1, 1942:

THERE SHALL BE NO WANT[1]

About eighteen months ago the government said to Sir William Beveridge, "Get together an interdepartmental committee and work out recommendations for uniting the various schemes of social insurance, including workmen's compensation." They also told him he could develop plans for death benefits and any other risks not covered by existing schemes. His job was to make

[1] The talks used as illustrations in this chapter are reprinted, by permission, from *Talks*, a quarterly digest of addresses published by Columbia Broadcasting System, Inc., New York.

a comprehensive survey of everything that's happened since the Poor Law was enacted 300 years ago.

The field was very broad, and, to Sir William, very inviting. For this eminent economist has spent more than thirty years studying such matters. He's a short, lean man of 63 with thin untidy gray hair and a large nose. He was mainly responsible for the creation of labor exchanges in this country and he has a terrific reputation for knowing all about employment, unemployment, and insurance.

The Beveridge report runs to 90,000 words, and there's a supplement of another 200,000 words. It isn't a law and it won't be for some time, if at all. The whole matter must be debated in the House of Commons. And there have been many reports that have failed to reach the statute books.

This is his report—a personal document, which in no way commits the government to the plans he purposes. But whether it's accepted or not, it will arouse lasting controversy. It gives form and substance to a dream, and whatever its fate, this report will rank as a great piece of scholarship, a great state paper. The issues are presented clearly in simple language and with a wealth of detail.

This is really a scheme to insure everybody for everything. It's the first domestic effort to translate part of the Atlantic Charter from words into deeds. It's a plan to abolish want in Britain. There are three main features:

First, all the existing schemes of social insurance—such as health, unemployment, old age, accident, and so forth, are to be combined into one scheme. By one single weekly contribution to a new Ministry of Social Security, everyone will be able to get all the benefits that he and his family need for as long as they need them. There will be family allowances so that all parents will have to keep their children strong and healthy, and they can have more children if they want them, without worrying too much about the cost.

There is also to be a comprehensive health service, guaranteeing medical treatment of all kinds for all citizens whether at home or in the hospital.   The plan covers everybody.   There are no upper income limits.   And the so-called "means" test, under which the individual had to prove an absence of personal financial resources, is abolished.   Sir William admits that his report is in some ways a revolution.   But he maintains that it is a national development from the past, a particular kind of British revolution.

The plan retains the system of contributions from workers, employers, and the state.   That principle was established by the National Health Act of 1911.   This comprehensive scheme aims at securing a healthier and happier Britain by giving each citizen an income adequate to satisfy minimum living standards. Employees will receive insurance against unemployment, disability, medical treatment, pension, and funeral services.   Employers, traders, and independent workers can't be insured against the loss of employment, but they will be provided for if they're disabled.   And they will be trained for new occupations if their livelihood is for any reason taken away.   The housewife will receive a marriage grant, a maternity grant, and special compensation if she has to give up paid work to have a child.   There will also be a provision for widowhood and separation.   People of private means—students and unmarried women doing domestic duties for which they are not paid—will receive medical treatment, retirement, and funeral expenses.   And they'll also be insured against the risk of having to find a new job.   Parents with children below the age of 16 will receive $1.60 a week for each child, excluding the first.   People above the working age will receive a pension on an increasing scale, which at the end of 20 years will amount to about $8 a week.   Workers who are totally disabled will be paid two-thirds of what they were earning.

One trouble with this country is that the number of old people is increasing.   In 1900 one person in 17 was of pensionable age, which is 65.   In 1931 it was one in 10.   And in 1961 it will be one in 6.   There is a need to increase the birthrate, and that's why the allowance for children is suggested.   It's also why the marriage grant will be about $40.   The maternity grant is $20.

And mothers who give up their jobs in order to have children will receive a little more than $7 a week for 13 weeks. The funeral grant may be as much as $80.

For all these benefits an adult man will be expected to contribute about $1 a week. His employer must provide about 75 cents each week. The way the whole thing works out is this: The contributions of employed people would represent about 25 per cent of the value of the cash payments they receive. The other 75 per cent would come from employers and the state. Children's allowances would come entirely from the state.

The total expenditure involved in this plan in 1945 would be roughly the amount of money Britain spends on two months of war. The new expenditure—that is, the amount over and above what is already spent on social services—would be 265,-000,000 pounds sterling. It costs that much to run the war for three weeks.

The rates of compensation are complicated and they may vary with the cost of living. But in general, a married man who is unemployed or disabled will receive $8 a week. And that's in addition to the allowance for his children, provision for medical service, and money to bury him. Unemployment insurance is unlimited as to time, but the man must attend a training center to learn a new job or a new trade if he's out of a job more than six months.

Sir William Beveridge thinks the scheme can begin operating on July 1, 1944, and that it will establish a national minimum above which prosperity can grow. He denies emphatically that it will give everybody something for nothing, since all will contribute. And he asserts that the decision should be taken during the war.

This report is a momentous document. It will hold out to people in this country the promise of a new Britain to be created by courage, faith, and unity. It will be useful in British propaganda aimed at the Continent. But it's a report, not a law. Many questions are still to be answered. The thing is full of political dynamite. The first reaction of the conservative newspapers has been cautious, emphasizing that the plan requires much study. But it has met with no full-blooded condemnation.

A committee of the War Cabinet will discuss his report and then it will come before Parliament. Tomorrow Sir William Beveridge will face an informal though predominantly conservative committee of the House of Commons.

Here are some of the questions he'll be expected to answer: "What happens to the insurance companies when everything is insured by the state?" The report has already caused their stock to slump on the London exchange. The doctors will want to know about their private practice if the state is to provide medical service. Some workers, such as miners, may want special treatment because their job is dangerous. Some sections of the industry will maintain that Britain's economic future may be too uncertain to warrant the making of such long-term commitments. The voluntary hospitals will be afraid of losing their supporters when the state provides hospital care.

There probably will be compromises, and certainly there will be much discussion. This report may produce the greatest political battle of the war. It will catch the imagination of the people. Whether it will catch the votes in Parliament remains to be seen. It is safe to predict that, when a general election is held, every candidate will be asked whether he is for or against the Beveridge report.

It has been announced at a good time. People are interested in postwar planning. Sir William understands politics as well as economics, for he says, "Decisions on principles should be taken now. The sense of national unity and readiness to sacrifice personal interests to the common cause makes possible changes difficult to make at other times." He concludes, "There appears to be no doubt of the determination of the British people —however hard-pressed in war—not to live wholly for war, not to abandon care for what may come after. That, after all, is in accord with the nature of democracy, of the spirit in which they fight and of the purpose for which they fight. What ever happens to this report—and it's meaningless without victory in a world where nations work together—it will give to many people here the hope that the youth of the country who went out to face death will not return to face unemployment and uncertainty."

May 29, 1943, Sir William Beveridge himself gave a report on his report. You may compare it with Mr. Murrow's report to discover differences in attitude and approach. Does Beveridge bring up an interesting point that Murrow overlooked? Why was Murrow's problem more complicated than Beveridge's?

FROM THE CRADLE TO THE GRAVE

My report proposes three things: First, a comprehensive scheme of social insurance for maintaining cash income when earning power is interrupted or comes to an end through any cause, whether it is sickness or accident or unemployment or old age or in the event a man dies.

Second, a comprehensive health service, which is meant to make certain that every citizen at all times when he's ill can get whatever medical treatment he needs to make him well again, without having to pay anything whatever at the time when he needs that treatment.

And then, there's a third part to the report which proposes cash allowances for children, not only when the father is out of work or sick but also when he's earning.

Our plan is social insurance and social insurance means premiums. There are really three parties to this business of paying premiums: the insured person, the employer—if the insured person has an employer—and the national government. We cannot insure the person who has no employer against unemployment, so he doesn't pay a premium for unemployment benefit. On the other hand, he pays what the insured person and the employer would pay together. All who are insured pay the same and all receive the same benefit, regardless of wages or of need.

It is a matter of self-respect. We think that if you pay a contribution, irrespective of your means, that's a good argument for getting a benefit irrespective of your means.

For a man and wife the unemployment pay should be something like 40 shillings a week. Actually that depends a little on what one expects prices to be. But if we assume prices to be after the war about 25 per cent above what they were before the war, on that basis I propose 40 shillings or about $8 a week for a man and wife. Then there would be children's allowances in addition. They would have by English standards just enough for absolute necessities.

With us it is fundamental that you should not cut down the money you give to a man when he is out of work or sick from the social insurance fund because he has managed to save something for himself. If you cut down what you give him from the social insurance fund because he has saved something for himself, you discourage him from saving; you destroy initiative, you destroy responsibility. If, on the other hand, you say, "In your old age, whatever other money you have got, you are certain of 40 shillings a week from this fund for yourself and your wife," I know of practically no one in Britain who would not say, "Well, I'd like to be a little better off and I'll try to save." He will know that he can keep his savings.

The benefit should last as long as the need lasts. Nobody should be unemployed indefinitely. The state ought to see that that does not happen, and further, there is a special proposal which I make, that if a man is to be unemployed for a certain length of time, he should be required to go to work for a training center, as a condition of benefit. That is because I think giving money to people for prolonged idleness is no real remedy for idleness. There is no danger of creating a nation of people that will not want to work. In any case, they would not have the chance, because the unemployment benefit, which incidentally is only a small part of the whole scheme, is administered through what we call employment exchanges. The man goes there and if a job is offered to him he cannot refuse that job and still get his benefit unless he can prove that he was reasonable in refusing. It may have been a job at a bad rate of wages or too far from his home or something of that sort.

What you do in this country with these problems is for you to decide. Quite definitely you have got the same problems. You have sick people, unemployed people, old people, people injured by accidents, breadwinners killed in this country, and you get, as a consequence, poverty in this country. We discovered, to our surprise in Britain, towards the end of the nineteenth century, that although we were so much richer than ever before, we also had a great deal of poverty. Well, now if you really look honestly at your own country, you will see that with an even higher standard of wealth you have also got a great deal of poverty. I think that the great value of your National Resources Planning Board Report is that it produces all the facts about the amount of unemployment in the states, the number of people in need of relief of different kinds, the black spots of almost permanent poverty that you have, and shows what will have to be taken care of in your own way.

There is nothing more down to earth than Beveridge's broadcast. He wastes no time in sparring for attention; tucks his report in a nutshell; assures you that government would not tolerate loafers and chronic idlers; reminds you that people will get their insurance because they pay for it, not because they need it; and notes that we in America, too, have a great deal of poverty that will compel us to improve our legislation for social security. You don't need any coaxing to take this plain stuff; indeed, you don't want any fancy trimmings on it. It's too serious. The man is talking about your life. He may be referring to Englishmen, but it is clear that the same sort of thing will happen over here.

Look at another example of unadorned exposition. Herbert Hoover has sometimes been accused of making long, learned-sounding speeches of large generalities but few specifications, but here is something from a speech of his before the American Farm Bureau Federation on June 8, 1943, that is a model of concise, direct, and concrete statement. Three short paragraphs of introduction preface his nine-point program. Each point flows naturally out of the one preceding it, and the few words of comment are impressive and convincing. Mr. Hoover has discovered the vital issues in the farm question, and his stating them so clearly and simply makes the correct solution seem relatively easy and not far away. Notice how much more effective a brief explanation can be as compared with complicated and somewhat acrimonious argument.

A REFORM IN FOOD CONTROL

There is only one course which will clear up this muddle of uncontrolled food prices, local famines, profiteering, black markets, and stifled farm production. That is to abandon the obsolete methods now in use which were proved a failure in other nations in the last war, or are copied from the British, whose situation is wholly different from ours. We should start with the system which proved a success under the Americans in the last war and improve it.

In the last war we steadily increased our food production. We shipped more food to our Allies monthly than is being shipped today. We had no local famines in the United States as we are having now, no black markets. We had a people zealous in a moral crusade to help win the war with food, instead of lots of people trying to beat the game. Including the Department of Agriculture, we had only 23,000 paid Federal employees connected with food. Today we have over 120,000. Moreover, food prices rose only 17.9 per cent in the 17 months after we declared war in 1917. Washington statisticians admit a rise of 24.3 per cent in the 17 months since Pearl Harbor. The housewives will admit a rise of at least 35 per cent.

I do not pretend that our methods were perfect in that war. We had to pioneer an unknown field. Results ought to be better in this war and not worse.

The first necessity is to consolidate all authority over food production and distribution under one single responsible administrator. The Food Administrator must today be the Secretary of Agriculture. And the importance of food in the outcome of the war and peace should be recognized by his appointment to the new Office of Manpower Mobilization.

Second. Decentralize the work under state, municipal, and county administrators.

Third. Increase the man power on the farms to a higher level than before the war and plant 40 to 50 million acres more in 1944 than in this year.

Public pressure on our farm boys to join the forces is very great. They are not slackers and do not want to be called slackers. They are doing a great and indispensable service. If we are to save this situation, I believe farm boys should be called to the army from the farms immediately after this harvest; that the farm boys should be called up from industry; that they should be given some military training. Then as many of them as are necessary should from time to time be ordered back to the farms with their uniforms. They should receive their pay from the farms, and not the army. They should be subject to call in national danger.

Fourth. Agricultural machinery on an average lasts about 12 years. Theoretically about one year's supply or one-twelfth of our machinery has been used up through suppression of manufacture. It will also require great additions to handle this extra 40 or 50 million acres in 1944.

Fifth. Abolish the system of retail and wholesale price ceilings. It begins at the wrong end. Price fixing in a great foodproducing country must begin as near as possible to the farmer and controls proceed from there on by regulation of the trades against profiteering. This present price system is stifling farm production. It is not stopping inflation.

Sixth. Ask the farmers to appoint their own war committee on prices and do a little collective bargaining with them in fixing prices. The so-called "parities" should be abandoned for the war. Prices to the farmer must include floors as well as ceilings. Prices should be fixed that will take into account labor and other costs, and above all that will stimulate production.

Seventh. Rations should be set to balance consumption to production. It only adds muddle to put the ration higher than the available supplies. And it brings great injustice, for some people get the ration and some don't. It can be done by decreasing the number and variety of articles rationed and by excluding all absolutely nonessential food from rationing.

Also a good way to check inflation is to let food luxuries go to the highest bidder. That would spigot off spare money and get it into channels where the 90 per cent profit taxes can bite into it.

Eighth. We should recognize that processing and distributing foods are righteous and necessary callings. Thousands of small firms are being driven out of business. It would help win the war if left-wing reforms in our economy were suspended for the duration. We should establish war committees in all the processing and distributing trades. They should be given major responsibilities in keeping the flow of food moving to the right spots. They could greatly assist state and local officials in policing the trades. They are the only people who know how. Their interest is to stamp out black markets. And their profits can be absolutely controlled.

Enforce the condition of dealers' licenses so that they may deal only with another licensed dealer and then direct the railways and trucks to transport only for licensed dealers. This would stop most of the black markets.

Ninth. Such a system will avoid subsidies either to farmers or trades or the consumers. Subsidies will not stop inflation. Subsidies are a delayed aggravation.

And who is supposed to benefit by subsidies? It is supposed to be the worker, but the worker is also the taxpayer. So is the farmer. And taxes are, sooner or later, increased by just the same amount as the subsidy. Subsidies consist of taking money out of one pocket and putting it into another with an illusion attached that the cost of living has been reduced.

A wage based on subsidy foundations will break down sooner or later. Moreover, subsidy money increases government borrowing and debt to the banks and that adds to inflation pressure. Far more serious, however, is the result to the farmer and the consumer. Price fixing based on any such concept will strangle production. Its operation in the distribution trades will clog the flow of commodities and will in the end increase prices and black markets. Likewise, subsidies can become a weapon of favoritism or of punishment in the hands of the huge bureaucracy. They will sooner or later lead to scandal.

Professional men are often asked to contribute a bit of their learning to radio audiences, and it is about this group that radio directors are most pessimistic. They fear the subjects will be dull, or that the speakers will let loose a barrage of technical jargon that will drive away the most willing listener.

Dr. Harry S. Gradle gave a talk in 1942 on glaucoma. He confined himself to what his audience would like to know and to what they could understand. He was informal and practical. He had just enough humor to be disarming, but he made an appeal to fear and to the necessity for prompt action. His persistent reference to "you" was arresting and "you" felt that you had better have this examination at once.

Any technical matter may have its vital meaning explained in clear and interesting talk. To fall back on the excuse that a subject cannot be explained to the layman because of the technical terminology involved is to confess ignorance, a certain muddleheadedness, about the topic one is expected to be master of. The subject can always be compared to something familiar, or defined by reference to items of common use. From the known to the unknown is still the teacher's surest formula. Answers to "So what?" give the talk its functional value and remove it from the academic to the practical plane. Dr. Gradle's strategy is to avoid getting difficult and tedious about the nature of his subject. He spends his time in telling why it is important to you and what you should do about it.

BEWARE OF GLAUCOMA

Glaucoma is a disease of the eyes, the cause of which has not yet been discovered. Until the war diverted our activities, the best brains in the world were working on that problem and still are in the few odd minutes that can be snatched from the war efforts.

Unless taken care of by medicine or surgery, glaucoma will cause complete blindness in nearly all cases. In fact, of the 120,000 people in these United States that are blind in both eyes, about 30,000 of them are blind as the result of glaucoma. Just stop for a minute and figure out what that means in hard cash. Every blind person without means is entitled to a blind pension of $1 a day, every day in the year as long as he or she lives. Thirty thousand people at $1 each day for the 365 days in the year, adds up to almost $1,000,000 a year that the taxpayer has to fork out, because the disease was not discovered in time. If glaucoma is discovered early and proper treatment started at once, less than 8 per cent of the eyes afflicted with glaucoma become blind.

If you are over forty, and you don't need to tell how much over, it will pay you to think about your eyes for a few minutes. If by chance you have glaucoma, you can save yourself many years of needless suffering, both mental and physical, by an early diagnosis and proper treatment.

The chances are that you need, or will need in the very near future, glasses for readin', writin', and 'rithmetic, not to mention sewing and gin rummy. Only about 20 per cent of you are going to go to an eye physician to get your glasses fitted. When you do, his routine examination of your eyes will pick up a glaucoma if it is present, even in an early stage. The next 40 per cent of you will get your glasses fitted by an optometrist or an optician. Many of these nonmedical refractionists are extremely skillful and can detect an early glaucoma; but unfortunately, the majority cannot. The remaining 40 per cent of you are going to buy glasses over the counter. So you see, about 80 per cent of all the people past forty who get glasses do not have the benefit of an examination that would detect the presence or absence of that disease known as glaucoma.

In his days in medical school, your doctor learned about the commoner diseases of the eye. But, in the hurly and the burly of a busy practice, he has not been able to keep in touch with the technical refinements that have developed in the various specialties. His patients have been given the benefit of those advances in knowledge by being referred through him to the various specialists, according to what was wrong with them. But now the eye specialists are going back to the family doctor and humbly asking his help to prevent the so unnecessary blindness from glaucoma by detecting that disease before it can do irreparable damage. And you, the patient of the family doctor, can be of enormous help to that cause by asking your doctor to make a cursory examination of your eyes as a part of his routine physical examination of your body. If you have glaucoma already developed, he will discover it. If you are threatened with glaucoma (and there is such a condition as pre-glaucoma), he will be suspicious and will send you to a specialist to confirm or refute his suspicions.

If you can, select a man who holds the certificate of the American Board of Ophthalmology, that certificate meaning that his fellow doctors recognize him as a competent eye physician.

Your eye physician will start by giving your eyes a thorough examination from front to back and inside and out.   All this may require several sittings.   Only after he knows all there is to know about your eyes will he outline the course of treatment. Now, every case of glaucoma is a law unto itself and no two people behave exactly the same with the various medicines that are used.   So it will take some little time for your eye physician to determine how your eyes react and just how much or how little treatment is required to hold the disease in check.

If you have glaucoma, you had better learn now than later that glaucoma cannot be cured, but can be arrested.   In other words, the disease will always be with you and the least slip in treatment on your part means danger for the future of your eyes. Unfortunately, glaucoma is not like a stomache ache, meaning that you can tell whether you have it or not, and only your eye physician can tell whether you or whether your glaucoma has the upper hand in the battle.

CHAPTER VIII

Writing Your Manuscript

By this time you can sympathize with the centipede who thought he was getting around pretty comfortably on his 100 legs. One day the toad stopped him and said, "How do you do it? Looks like quite a trick to keep all those feet going, and out of each other's way. Which foot do you put down first? Which next?" He kept up this chatter while the centipede tried patiently to unravel the process. What he did spontaneously, without effort or thought, now became a baffling riddle. Instead of walking he was trying to understand and explain the theory of walking. He spent a long time trying to figure all this out. Then, when he wanted to get going according to the diagram he had composed with such worry and labor, the poor fellow found that he couldn't walk at all.

Reading advice and directions about doing things affects us like that. What was easy suddenly becomes difficult and confused. What we did by instinct we now are told to do by rule. At any rate, the old dash over the one-way route is over. There are choices, new lines, approaches, and attitudes to be pondered. They make us self-conscious, slow us up, and discourage us with their variety of distracting suggestions.

This awareness is the painful birth of your new order of thinking and composing. It warns you of the things you shouldn't do and questions your taste and judgment. It helps you to discover important matters that you had over-looked. It begins to create a more mature and flexible style.

Well, with your outline before you, sit down and write. Don't worry too much about individual words and phrases. You are going to revise your first copy and will think of plenty of improvements. You know, a speech grows, changes its shape and texture, with your own active and progressive thinking. Writing is not easy. For most people, it's the hardest part of radio speaking. And sometimes they get so fascinated with what they have put on paper that they don't want to alter it.

Fortunately, there is one thing that usually makes it necessary. You have to fit your material almost exactly into a given time scheme. If you are on a 15-minute program your talk should take about 11½ minutes to read at a moderately paced, conversational gait. Time must be allowed for the announcer to introduce you, as well as to make his closing remarks.

When you have completed the writing of your speech, read it aloud and have a member of the family check the time carefully. Have you got to add paragraphs or take them out? Use all your available time, if possible. The announcer, or director, can, if necessary, fill in time left over, by playing a record, but that is always a sign of poor management, and the studio would prefer not to be put to that confession.

On the other hand, if your talk is too long you may be cut off in the middle of a sentence. Time on the air is scheduled by seconds, and you are not allowed to take the time of another program. It often happens that a speech may be several paragraphs too long even when it has been carefully timed in rehearsal. The speaker may unintentionally change his rate of speed, speak more carefully, more slowly, and so not finish in time.

For this emergency he should always have at least two short paragraphs, near the end of his talk, that he could leave out without violating the clearness or continuity of his talk. When he gets to his last page, he should look up at the director to see whether he is giving the sign to cut. He does this by drawing a finger across his throat. That is the cue to skip a few lines and conclude promptly.

It sounds troublesome but really isn't. If you have taken reasonable precautions, the announcer can handle the situation comfortably. He has a few seconds of latitude. He can speed up his own reading a bit, or slow down a little, to close neatly at the right moment.

Your manuscript should, of course, be neatly typed in double space. You should not handicap yourself with penmanship or type that is not easy to read. Some speakers time themselves very carefully and note in the margin at the bottom of each page the minutes and seconds consumed up to that point. With this precaution they can know, when they are on the air, how closely they are observing the determined rate of speaking.

In revising your script you naturally speculate about the effectiveness of individual words. Have a good desk dictionary always at hand to make sure of pronunciations and to find synonyms that may express a shade of meaning more accurately. Of course you want picture words and action words. What sort of place did John Smith live in? *House* is too vague a word. Did he live in a *cottage* or a *bungalow* or a *shack* or a *parsonage* or a *palace?* When he went out of the room did he *steal*, or *glide*, or *creep*, or *stumble*, or *swagger*, or *dash*, or *rush*, or *dance*, or *slouch*, or *shamble*, or *slip*, or *stride* out?

" 'Go,' she said." The picture is faint. *Said* lacks description. Perhaps she *urged, screamed, pleaded, cried, murmured, sighed, exclaimed,* or *commanded.*

Of course, if previous details in the context have already made a good picture, *said* may be just the right word—simple and direct. Some of our sophisticated novelists give us bizarre substitutes for *said.* Here is a clever bit of newspaper verse that is a good lesson in the advantage of synonyms and in the danger of overrefinement, a very slight one in the case of most speakers:

SAID

"Thank you, kind sir," she sweetly said—
　But *said,* we're told, is obsolete.
The modern hero, thoroughbred,
　Would stoop to nothing so effete.
He states, affirms, declares, asserts,
He whispers, murmurs, booms, and blurts;
He rumbles, and mumbles, and grumbles, and snorts,
He answers, replies, rejoins, and retorts—
　But never by any chance *says.*
He hisses, wheezes, whines, and howls,
He husks and brusques, he grunts and growls.
He (horrors!) *nasals,* yells, and wails,
He warns and scorns, he rails and quails—
　But *says?* O, no!
He grants, admits, agrees, assents,
Concedes, and even compliments,
He challenges, regrets, denies,
Evades, equivocates, and lies—
　And *says?* Not so.
He wanders and ponders, considers and wonders,
He speculates, calculates, puzzles, and blunders,
He argues and quibbles, defends or accuses,

Accepts, acquiesces, or flouts and refuses—
    But *says?*—Pooh pooh!
He flutters, worries, rants, and tears,
He sparkles, flashes, blazes, flares;
He chuckles, grins, and cachinnates,
He gloats, exults, and jubilates—
    But *says?*—Taboo!
O, shades of Thackeray and Scott,
    Of Kipling and that hapless throng,
All born untimely! Bitter thought:
    They never knew that *said* was wrong!
       H. M. KINGERY, in *The New York Evening Post.*

Sometimes you want a synonym, not because your first selection isn't good enough but because you don't like to repeat it. You think it sounds clumsy and tiresome to use the same word over and over again. This attitude is sound in the case of many words, but be sure the substitutions are natural and not forced. It is better to repeat the names and terms of necessary things and operations than to beat about the bush for roundabout and farfetched synonyms. It isn't necessary to imitate the style of the sports writer. He doesn't call a ball a *ball*. He calls it the *apple*, the *agate*, the *pill*, the *horsehide*. In football it isn't enough that the halfback *ran:* he *slid, breezed, slithered, galloped, thundered, wriggled, slammed,* or *punched* through the line. We know that much of this is nonsense but we appreciate the fact that the reporter is looking for variety and doesn't want to wear us out with *ran*.

Now it seems rather odd that when repetition is accidental it is dull and fatiguing but that when it is planned it is likely to be forceful. Here, in the opening paragraph of a speech by Governor Dixon of Alabama, you get a good illustration. The words repeated for emphasis are italicized:

Democracy is not a thing of Washington. *Democracy* is a *thing* of the crossroads. It is at the *crossroads* that the people of this nation live. *It* is at the *crossroads* that their children are born, *that* they go to church on Sunday, *that* the schools are placed, *that* the average American citizen lives his life and is finally taken to his fathers. *It is at the crossroads* that the life of America takes place—not in Washington. Let his local officials become overly ambitious and interfere with his rights, he knows it immediately and acts. *Let any local* dictator seek to establish himself, *he knows it immediately*, and the methods and the means to strike that man down are in his hands. The base of democracy is there, *there* it will endure or die. *There* it is strong, tenacious of life, resistant to degeneration or decay.

This sort of repetition is associated almost solely with the art of oratory or persuasion. It is seldom a helpful device in unemotional explanation or description. But see how vividly *crossroads* stands out in contrast to *Washington*. Observe the inverted repetition of "The base of democracy is there, *there* it will endure." The rhythm and balance are more noticeable because unusual, and yet they are pleasing to the ear. When this trick of rhetoric is not overdone, it is an easy method of getting and holding attention.

Your style will improve when you recognize dead spots and rub them out. Clichés, stale fancy phrases, are the deadest, or, at least, the most tiresome. The trouble is, you won't always notice them. Nobody does remove them entirely from his vocabulary because there are too many. That isn't the chief cause, however. It's quite likely that you are fond of certain of these trite expressions that experts in style insist you should avoid. They were once good, but they have now lost their savor. Here is a list that will remind you of many others:

add insult to injury
act in cold blood
agree to disagree
age before beauty
alive and kicking
all and sundry
ample opportunity
armed to the teeth
at the psychological moment
battle royal
beaten track
between the devil and the deep blue sea
bitter irony
blank amazement
bundle of nerves
call a halt
care a rap
crack of doom
conspicuous by their absence
do or die
dyed in the wool
each and every
full of sound and fury
it may interest you to know
know the ropes
man in the street
moral victory
null and void
overwhelming odds
picture of health
pure and simple
royal road
rank treason
shot one's bolt
sickening thud
supreme sacrifice

sweat of one's brow
to all intents and purposes
vicious circle
wishful thinking
without rhyme or reason
your earliest convenience

These were once eloquent bits. They got attention and people repeated them. They've had a long run, longer than *Uncle Tom's Cabin* or *Tobacco Road*, and it's time we put most of them away. We are certainly a lot of second-raters if we must forever twang away with these ancient quips and cracks. Must the track always be beaten, the irony bitter, the amazement blank, the odds overwhelming, the thud sickening, and the circle vicious? Perish the thought! (Excuse us, we can't get away from the damn things.)

There is no end to this study. The language seems like a great rubbish heap of played-out terms. Think of the similes no thoughtful person would dare use now. Begin with this small list and add others that you can easily dig up:

brown as a berry
bull in a china shop
caught like a rat in a trap
cool as a cucumber
dying like flies
easy as falling off a log
flat as a pancake
old as Methuselah
quick as a flash
sharp as a razor
silent as the grave
swear like a trooper

like a ton of bricks
warm as toast
white as a sheet

Figures of speech are necessary. They are more vivid forms of comparison and contrast, and the most effective way of defining or describing anything is by comparing it with something else, something thoroughly familiar to everybody. Occasionally these fossilized figures of speech are thoughtlessly mixed up and become funny. If you hear someone say, "The underdog is in the saddle," you know what he means, but the literal picture is a kind of nightmare. You see the chewed-up dog at the bottom of the barking, yelping, dusty confusion suddenly put on a horse. In fact he's in a saddle and you expect him to fall off any moment. That situation may be possible, but try to find some logic in this pippin quoted by L. T. Townsend in *The Art of Speech:*

Gentlemen: The apple of discord has been thrown into our midst; and if it be not nipped in the bud, it will burst into a conflagration that will deluge the world.

Scott Fitzgerald said he found this Irish, or American, bull in the Congressional Record:

I seem to see Columbia blindfolded, covered with scales, driving the ship of State over the battlefields of the Republic into the heart of the Golden West and the cotton fields of the Sunny South.

That is what is liable to happen to any person who gets so enamored of the sounds of words that he gives little heed to their sense.

But we are always in search of the fruitful comparison. If we can't find it in a phrase we may discover it in a paragraph or two of definition, of turning the object around and around until we see something that reminds us of that other thing that will make everything clear or exciting to our listeners. Examine this stimulating example that begins with the general and vague word *port*. With a bit of focusing the speaker dispels the mist and reveals a rich and detailed landscape. Notice, in the second paragraph, how he has hit upon just the right comparison to make the size of the port something you wouldn't have considered possible, and something, therefore, that you'll always remember.

The word *port* is generally regarded as synonymous with a single harbor on which is situated some single city. The Port of New York, unlike any other on this continent if not in the world, has not less than six distinct harbors—the Lower and Upper Bays, Newark Bay, Jamaica Bay and Flushing Bay and Raritan Bay, each one almost as large as any ordinary harbor, and all connected by a series of sheltered waterways which together furnish shore lines about nine hundred miles in length, and the Port District embraces 105 separate municipalities, of which about half border directly on some portion of the waters of the Port. One of these municipalities is Newark, with about four hundred and twenty thousand population, where this splendid broadcasting station is located.

Traveling 10 hours a day on a vessel of 10 knots speed, it would take 8 days merely to coast along the shore lines of the waters of the Port, or the average time of a fast transatlantic steamer on a voyage to Europe. If stretched out along the Atlantic Coast, New York's water front would reach almost from Charleston, S.C., to Boston, and in a westerly direction on an air line, it would extend from New York to a point more than 100 miles west of Chicago.

EUGENE HARVEY OUTERBRIDGE.

Check these items before you finish writing your script:

1. Does your opening sentence suggest something of interest to the listener?

2. Are the sentences short and yet varied in length?

3. Does the script sound like talk?

4. Are there enough transitional words and phrases, such things as, "There is, however, another side to this matter," "on the other hand," "nevertheless," "but this is not all," etc.?

5. Are the paragraphs short and coherent? Do they indicate progressive and logical steps of development?

6. Is your last sentence a summary, a challenge, an invitation, a spur to action, a quotation, a question, or an indication of good will after argument or controversy?

CHAPTER IX

The Radio Round Table

Extemporaneous discussion is a pleasure to some speakers, a nightmare to others. If you are full of your subject, so familiar with it that you enjoy a cheerful argument with two or three others about it, you may prefer the round table because you don't have to write a painstaking script and stick to it on the air. Of course, it's one thing to talk in private and something else to be heard by listening thousands. If your public is actually only four or five families, the effect on your blood pressure is just the same.

The round table, without proper preparation is, indeed, a hazardous and fearful business, and of little profit to the listener. How often the speakers get lost in a fog of explanation or argument, or dawdle with a minor point so long that they are left talking to themselves! One speaker, in an orderly 5-minute talk, can accomplish more than three who get tangled up in aimless, planless, 15-minute rigmarole.

But discussion can be more vital and informative than speechmaking. In considering controversial issues the participants cannot dodge important or embarrassing questions. They cannot escape into oratory or specious disposal of difficult problems. They must be prepared at every step to answer the challenge of *what*, *why*, and *how*.

Discussion is democratic and direct. Its purpose is not to discover facts but to interpret them. It differs from propaganda and persuasion because it compares proposed solutions and remedies and tries to find the most useful and practicable. In theory it is cooperative in the search for truth, not competitive or committed to one side, as is debate. Of course, when a representative of capital meets a representative of labor in a round table, the public relations attitude cannot be entirely dropped. Each is conscious that his crowd is listening and will resent his admitting too much or compromising too readily. Nevertheless, even when prominent persons are brought together just because they represent clashing opinions, they try to keep the discussion on a plane of objective, intelligent reasoning. They know that any attempt to get away from the down-to-earth and courteous atmosphere of good talk by slipping into the evasive devices of oratorical whim-wham will be a fatal confession of weakness.

Not all discussion programs are controversial. Dialogue is essentially dramatic, and when it is good it will hold the attention better than a monologue. Notice how the advertisers have tried to exploit this fact in interviews, testimonials, playlets—anything that will bring another voice beside the announcer's into the commercial. Many round tables are merely more entertaining vehicles of information about books, politics, people, and the war.

The method may be sound, but in practice it is often hard to prove. Three dull and indifferent speakers are not so good as one alert and methodical speaker. Plans and rehearsals make a great deal of difference.

Imagination, too, is needed. Nothing is more exasperating than to hear speakers laboriously thresh old straw. Not everything needs defining and explaining. People in the audience read newspapers and magazines and have the background for popular questions. They have a right to expect reasonable dispatch in disposing of preliminaries, and a clear, concise treatment of the significant issues.   In a discussion about the Balkans, for instance, every audience, at this writing, wants expert opinion on these questions:

Would it be good policy now to attack Germany through the Balkans?

What objection, if any, does Russia have to this strategy?

Can anything be done to form a cooperative union of the Balkan States?

Should they be allowed complete independence?

Should they be subject to Russia?

Should they have domestic independence but be subject in their foreign relations to control by a commission of the United Nations?

If too much time is spent in discussing the age-old traditions, prejudices, and feuds of these countries, in telling why Serbs can't get along with Croats, why Hungarians hate Rumanians, and so on, the proposed solutions of these problems will have to be neglected.   And it won't make the audience feel any better to be told at the end of the period that lack of time prevented the speakers from taking up those matters the audience has been patiently waiting for.

Every radio round table should have a leader if for no other reason than seeing that a schedule is followed.   The members should have a preliminary meeting to discuss the nature of their coming discussion.   After they have mapped out their course of procedure they should try out their discussion just as if they were on the air.   Each member may have notes and questions that fit into the main scheme, and the leader, who takes as much part in the discussion as the others, asks the leading questions if necessary.   He also sees that no topic is considered beyond its allotted number of minutes, and allows himself a minute or two at the close of the period to summarize conclusions.

The rehearsal will disclose any lack of necessary facts and will suggest a pattern for the more fluent and precise delivery that will go on the air. Without memorizing anything the speakers achieve a greater confidence, ease, and assurance, much as a salesman does after his first two or three skirmishes with "prospects." They have also the added advantage of making notes to bring to the discussion and of writing down items during the progress of the talk, hints that give them cues for continued effective participation.

Controversial questions always deal with problems, obstacles to our personal comfort or to our better social life. It is said that difficulties alone make us think, that in the placid round of routine activities we go to sleep mentally. It is only when something interferes with our easygoing habits that we awake to awareness, stop to examine the unwelcome and irritating nuisance, and try to dispose of it or get round it.

The process of reflective thinking has often been analyzed. John Dewey, in *How We Think*, has reduced it to five distinct steps. The first is a *felt difficulty*. Something is troubling us enough to get our sustained attention. The second step is its *location and definition*. Where is it and what is it? This step may require a good deal of analysis, a study of the background of conditions and causes. It is the diagnosis the doctor must make before he can write the prescription.

The third step is the *suggestion of possible solution*. What can we do about it? Often the diagnosis suggests several possible solutions. So the fourth step is the *development by reasoning of the bearings of the suggestion*. The same facts will be interpreted differently and the logic of debate and disagreement may only obscure the best remedy.

The fifth step, says Dewey, is "further observation and experiment leading to its [the proposed solution] acceptance or rejection; that is the conclusion of belief or disbelief." Now, the observation and experiment of science or business management may allow an inexpensive testing, but in the social and political world it is hard to retrace steps. Measures and practices cannot be easily repealed. Note the history of the Prohibition Amendment. A solution that seems perfect in theory may work out badly in practice.

Dewey's outline of the process of thought emphasizes, however, the element of discovery in the search for truth. It implies the honest, patient examination of facts that is not deterred by tradition or prejudice. It stresses reason and logic and diminishes the force of wishful thinking and personal preference.

Nevertheless, as a pragmatic philosopher, Dewey fully recognizes the pressure of politics, dogmas, and creeds. The scientific method is based on the democratic principle of freedom of thought and speech, but it cannot operate effectively in the social and political affairs of a country unless there is considerable "improvement of the methods and conditions of debate, discussion and persuasion." Dewey regards that as "*the* need of the public."

Though preparation, progress, and production should be the watchword of discussion on the air, the quality and atmosphere of the talk will naturally vary with the character and training of the speakers. The most earnest perform-ance may still be dull if the warmth and ease of informal, spontaneous talk is lacking. The plan must be flexible as well as orderly. It should have room for unexpected but brief diversions and clashes that may be entertaining or illuminating.

Every speaker has definite responsibilities to the group and to his audience. These do not require that he subdue his personality to a colorless carefulness. He may have to forgo some of the boisterous insult and badinage that so commonly enlivens the talk of intimates, but that is no reason for suppressing a sense of playfulness and humor. He need only remind himself that the few common rules of good private talk had better be more thoughtfully observed in public talk.

The first requirement of discussion is congenial spirit. In controversy disagreement furnishes the drama—the excitement, suspense, and discovery for the audience. The speakers should welcome their necessary conflicts of opinion as the things that make the show. Stiff manners, suspicious attitudes, overeagerness for a personal triumph will ruin what should be a cooperative effort to please and enlighten the public.

The secret of success in argument lies in the disarming approach. Don't get yourself out on a limb. Don't commit yourself so irrevocably to a fixed point of view that you can't retreat or admit weakness in your position without losing face. You are expected to invite the help of your colleagues in finding the best solution and should present your material as contributing and clarifying analysis, argument, and question.

Don't challenge your colleagues with phrases like "That's all wrong," "That's a superficial argument," "If you'd studied a recent government survey you wouldn't say that," "Anybody with a little experience in business knows that's impossible." Such beginnings spoil the excellent remarks that may follow. They give offense to the audience as well as to the person addressed.

It is just as easy to say, "I suppose most people feel that way about it, but there's one thing I can't reconcile with it. This is what I have in mind." Or, "Here is a point of view that I think we ought to consider," "Can we overlook this common criticism?" "Don't you think we have to examine the premises of that argument a little more closely?" "Haven't we overlooked an important point?" "That's well put but I think we still have to meet this objection."

When Benjamin Franklin was a young man he had an irritating trick of humiliating opponents by his superior wit and logic. He soon discovered that while he was winning arguments he was losing friends and supporters for measures he was advocating. He set out deliberately to change his manner and habit and became America's most influential salesman and diplomat. A paragraph from his *Autobiography* is as enlightening as any modern chapter on persuasion. He says:

[I retained] only the habit of expressing myself in terms of modest diffidence, never using, when I advance anything that may possibly be disputed, the words *certainly, undoubtedly,* or any others that give the air of positiveness to an opinion; but rather say, *I conceive,* or *apprehend,* a thing to be so and so; *It appears to me,* or *I imagine it to be so;* or *It is so, if I am not mistaken.* This habit, I believe, has been of great advantage to me when I have had occasion to inculcate my opinions and persuade men into measures that I have been from time to time engaged in promoting. And as the chief ends of conversation are to inform or to be informed, to please or persuade, I wish well-meaning and sensible men would not lessen their power of doing by a positive assuming manner, that seldom fails to disgust, tends to create opposition, and to defeat most of those purposes for which speech was given to us. In fact, if you wish to instruct others, a positive dogmatical manner in advancing your sentiments may occasion opposition, and prevent a candid attention. If you desire instruction and improvement from others, you should not at the same time express yourself fixed in your present opinions. Modest and sensible men, who do not love disputation, will leave you undisturbed in the possession of your errors. In adopting such a manner, you can seldom please your hearers, or obtain the concurrence you desire. Pope judiciously observes,

> Men must be taught, as if you taught them not,
> And things unknown proposed as things forgot.

On the other hand, don't be too cautious. Don't beat about the bush in your desire to be pleasant. Be frank, direct, sincere. It is true that most people who boast that they are frank are only "fresh" instead of refreshing. Good talk is animated by the speakers who come to the point, who declare themselves in neat, stimulating but smiling fashion.

Conciseness is, of course, essential. Agreeable conversation implies tossing the ball of talk around and letting everybody have a reasonable share in it. Long-windedness is a defect of many otherwise excellent speakers. Their fluency only makes them ineffective and tiresome. They forget that others wish to speak and are merely waiting impatiently to get in a few words of their own. Speeches should be limited to a minute or two.

You have no doubt often noticed another fault of speakers—that of interrupting to correct or refute a statement. This overeagerness betrays weakness, a lack of poise. It is a discourtesy that listeners at once resent. Patient, attentive listening is not only better etiquette but it also helps to organize a cooler, clearer, more incisive reply.

These rather obvious cautions remind us that the leader of the discussion can do a great deal to ensure harmony and progress. He is not a dictator but, seated in the middle, he can tactfully direct the course of the talk. If speakers get overheated he can pleasantly ask a question, insert a conciliatory comment to relieve the tension, or end the argument by simply reminding the group that it is time to take up another topic.

If one of the speakers is not taking part enough, the leader may address him by name and give him a cue for easy response. If the talk becomes irrelevant or unproductive the leader should get the group back to the planned procedure.

All this should be done as unobtrusively as possible. The audience need not suspect that there is a leader unless the introductory remarks and the summary at the end of the broadcast give some indications. The leader should be as active as the others in the talk, and they should be as responsible as he for its orderly, effective progress, but it is safer to have one member of the round table keep a supervisory eye and ear on things.

In the specimen round table that follows, you have an opportunity to study the characteristic virtues and defects of radio discussion. It is very interesting and yet somewhat disappointing. The men who composed the round table had such conflicting views to express that this meeting was a "natural." William Benton, the leader, has been vice-president of the University of Chicago since 1937, but for years he was in the advertising business and was well known through the Benton and Bowles Agency. Eric A. Johnston is president of the United States Chamber of Commerce and has been attracting much favorable attention by his articles and speeches. Harold J. Laski is a scholar of world-wide reputation. A "left-winger" often classified as a Communist, he is professor of political science at the University of London and at the London School of Economics. He has spent many years in America, where he has taught at Harvard, Yale, and McGill. Busy as he has been with books and articles he still has found time to be active in politics, and is a member of the National Executive Committee of the English Labour Party.

Benton and Johnston, at the time this round table was arranged, were in England to study English business methods and the attitudes of English businessmen toward the postwar problems of business. They found, incidentally, much greater complacency about, and even considerable approval of, government "planned economy" and control.

This discussion might have given us valuable comment on specific problems, but the speakers stuck to generalities. Laski was beaten down by the combined speeches of Benton and Johnston. Although Laski said early in the broadcast, when Benton remarked that the Americans might be taking advantage of the English Socialist, "Oh, do not worry about that. I feel equal to both of you put together," he did not get much beyond a delaying rear-guard action. He asked some difficult questions, got patronizing on occasion, and accused Johnston of "pure rhetoric,"—bunk, on the other side of the tracks. There was humor, some irrelevant byplay about dreams, nightmares, and a couple of metaphors.

Laski objected to Johnston's use of the word *regimentation* and said it was "intentional and used for the purpose of importing prejudice into this argument." Talk is full of blanket words emotionally charged that need to be defined and reduced to specific instances. Johnston mentioned the word *monopoly*, which Laski denied using.

The speakers tried to avoid phrases, labels, name calling, which affect the public more powerfully than careful, honest examination and reasoning from admitted facts. It is so much easier to toss around terms like *reactionary, radical, free enterprise, rugged individualism, Wall Street, corporate interests, efficiency, paternalism, communism,* and other metaphors and abstractions that may be misleading and deceptive or that may mean nothing.

You might begin the study of semantics, "the science of meanings," by reading Stuart Chase's *The Tyranny of Words.* At least you will form the habit of recognizing these "snarl words" and "purr words" for what they are.[1]

The round table was lively and stimulating, even though there was little discussion of the obvious difficulties in maintaining the necessary high level of employment after the war. The talk showed plan and systematic progress from point to point. Mr. Benton began with a good introduction, and his first question brought from Mr. Laski a neat, concise statement of "the heart of the problem." Mr. Benton summarized from time to time, indicating points of agreement, and closed with an accurate and forceful statement of "the core of the problem" and the conflicting points of view presented. A brisk fluency as well as precision characterized the language of the speakers, and the forward motion and tension easily held the interest to the end.

Examine the script carefully for passages that may have been written out and read at the appropriate cue. This is good procedure if it doesn't get too complicated and if it sounds like spontaneous reply or comment. Certainly the leader may get some comfort out of the sprightly paragraphs

[1] See S. I. Hayakawa, *Language in Action,* p. 59, Harcourt, Brace and Company, New York.

he has prepared in advance for his opening and closing remarks.

THE ECONOMIC SYSTEM—TODAY AND TOMORROW[1]

MR. BENTON: History is moving so fast these days that I do not think that we can tell, as we sit around this microphone in London, how important today is going to be in the histories of our countries.

I *do* know that today is the most significant and interesting day in the history of the University of Chicago Round Table. The Round Table has been broadcasting each week for over twelve years, but this is the first program ever broadcast outside the United States. We are here in the British Broadcasting Corporation studios, two floors underground, in what can be called a bombproof shelter.

I do not think that the three of us could have a more vital or important subject today. Our economic system interests everyone everywhere, and it is of particular interest to Johnston and me because that is why we are in London. As, at long last, we begin to win the war, it is going to become not only more important but more immediate.

Laski, what do you regard as the heart of this problem? How can we begin to diagnose it simply?

MR. LASKI: Full employment is the heart of the problem. Without full employment I do not see how it is possible to dream of maintaining democratic governments after the war.

MR. BENTON: Do you agree with that, Johnston?

MR. JOHNSTON: Next to war, mass unemployment is the most insidious, the most corroding, and the most devastating malady of our generation. We must learn to cure it by learning as much about mass distribution as we now know about mass production.

[1] Given in cooperation with the National Broadcasting Company August 15, 1943. Reprinted, by permission, from *The University of Chicago Round Table*, No. 282.

I do not agree with the use of the term "full employment" because I do not know what Laski means by full employment.

MR. BENTON: A phrase which I prefer, rather than Laski's, is "high levels of employment." Full employment is very hard to define. The phrase "full employment" promises, it seems to me, more than we should expect any economic system to perform. The performance might even be unhealthy. I think that the objective of the economic system should be high and satisfactory levels of employment.

MR. LASKI: I am a peaceful person, and, as long as your level is high enough, I shall not quarrel with you about that.

MR. BENTON: Then I guess that all three of us agree upon that point, but there is one other point as well—the level of production. That, in turn, depends on technological skills and on hours of labor. Certainly, we could secure high levels of employment by dropping the hours of work from 40 to, say, 20 hours each week, or we could secure high levels of employment by trying to build, let us say, a Boulder Dam with hand shovels. Such an approach to employment would provide the jobs all right, but it would be decreasing production and would actually make us a race of paupers at the end of it.

MR. LASKI: Of course, I agree that a high level of employment, as you call it, must involve a high level of production, and a high level of production which requires continuous technological development determines the standard of life.

Mr. BENTON: Johnston, do you think that more people are going to want jobs after the war rather than fewer?

MR. JOHNSTON: I am sure that we are going to have to find jobs in the United States for some fifteen or sixteen million more people after the war than before. The point is that American industry is being called upon to provide jobs for more and more workers. For instance, millions of women who never worked before this war are now employed in the war industries. Many of them will want to, and I believe that they should, be employed after the war.

MR. BENTON: One reason for that, of course, is the rapid set-up in technological techniques which has taken place in our country as well as in yours. At the production levels of 1940, the highest ever achieved in the United States, we turned out one hundred billion dollars in goods and services. That same production level after the war, in line with these modern developments in technology, would thus result in fifteen million unemployed in the United States.

I guess that we have agreed about the heart of the problem—the economic system must aim at high levels of employment and production. Are we talking about the economic systems of our own countries or the economic system of the world?

MR. LASKI: I suggest that we should illustrate from the United States and from England, because quite obviously the three of us know conditions there very much better than we know them elsewhere.

MR. BENTON: We hope so.

MR. LASKI: But I suggest, also, that whatever principles apply to the United States and England apply generally. We cannot separate our economic problems from the problems of the rest of the universe. That is what T. V. Soong, the Chinese minister of finance, meant when he told us in London, last Sunday, of the coming industrialization of China after victory.

MR. BENTON: The three of us seem to agree on the diagnosis. Our disagreements, I am sure, are going to begin with the prescription.

Laski, as a member of the Executive Committee of the Labour party here in England and as a self-identified left-wing Socialist, I am sure that you will disagree with Johnston and me on the prescription.

MR. LASKI: No doubt.

MR. BENTON: Johnston is here in London as president of the United States Chamber of Commerce, representing the million American businesses which belong to the Chamber. I am here as the vice-chairman of the recently formed Committee for Economic Development, which is dedicated to the achievement of high levels of employment and production after the war.

Laski, suppose you give Johnston and me your prescription to apply against the diagnosis on which all three of us have agreed.

MR. LASKI: The essence of the problem is planned production for community consumption; that is my prescription for you and Johnston.

MR. BENTON: Planned production by the state?

MR. LASKI: By the state.

MR. BENTON: What's your diagnosis, Johnston?

MR. JOHNSTON: I believe that, in order to increase employment and maintain freedom and opportunity for all our people, we must unleash the initiative and the driving force inherent in the millions of our people. I certainly have a greater confidence in the initiative of millions, which a free economy generates, than I do in the theoretical judgment of just a few bureaucrats who are at the top. This initiative of the millions will be accompanied by an expanding economy and by vastly increasing production all over the world. It follows that the increase in production will guarantee new high levels of employment—levels never even dreamed of before. This, in my opinion, is the American businessman's conception of the free and the dynamic future.

MR. BENTON: The difference between Laski, on the one hand, and you and me, on the other (and I agree with you, Johnston, so perhaps we are taking advantage of Laski here) . . . .

MR. LASKI: Oh, do not worry about that. I feel equal to both of you put together.

MR. BENTON: I guess that that is an example of English hospitality.

MR. LASKI: No. English self-assurance.

MR. BENTON: . . . is that we draw the line of difference on the prescription between what perhaps can be called by you, Laski, government enterprise, planned and directed by the state, and individual enterprise, on the other, advocated by Johnston and me.

MR. LASKI: May I put a question to you two at once? If you and Johnston think that private enterprise is going to be so much more beneficial after this war than it was after the last, how do you account for the fact that we went from the last war straight into the depression of 1929?

MR. BENTON: Johnston, I'm going to pass that question over to you.

MR. JOHNSTON: Laski, you know that it is not true that the level of increase of production took us straight into the depression of 1929. I am amazed that a man like you would make a statement of that kind. It was, perhaps, the maldistribution of the production. We are finding out in the United States today that there is no such thing as overproduction.

MR. BENTON: Let me handle that from another angle for Laski. We use phrases like "private enterprise" in a very loose way. The private enterprise system of our country, and your country, too, has, to an appreciable extent, in the last 20 or 30 years perhaps not been sufficiently private or even perhaps sufficiently enterprising. The private enterprise system so called has been actually on the retreat for decades. As we get down later in our discussion, Johnston, I think that we should examine, at greater length, just what we mean by a private enterprise system that will do this job. But suppose you elaborate, Laski, on what you think the role of the state in the economy should be.

MR. LASKI: Of course, I am a Socialist—what you called "a self-identified left-wing Socialist."

MR. BENTON: Pretty good phrase.

MR. LASKI: I am convinced that the effective direction of the whole of enterprise in your country and in ours—in any society, that is to say—is best operated by the state on behalf of the society.

MR. JOHNSTON: Now let me ask you if you mean direction by the state such as we had in Germany, for instance, before this war? Is that the kind of an institution you would want?

MR. LASKI: No, you know that it is not such as we had in Germany before the war.

MR. JOHNSTON: It was directed by the state, wasn't it?

MR. LASKI: Yes, but you *also* know that it was not directed by the state for the benefit of the mass of the community, and I defined that purpose as the one that I had in view—that Socialists have in view—as planned production for community consumption.

MR. JOHNSTON: That is what always happens when the state directs. It is never for the benefit of the mass of the people but always for a small group of the bureaucratic elite. Our industry is always planned in America. I have more confidence in the planning of millions than I do in the planning of a few, such as you recommend. All you want to do is to transfer the ownership and the direction from the many to the few.

MR. LASKI: Nonsense, Johnston. On your next visit to London I would like to give you a short course in American economic history.

MR. JOHNSTON: If you ever come to the United States, I might give you a short course on business which really produces and makes jobs.

MR. BENTON: I would like to attend both courses. Laski claims, Johnston, the right to define what he means by state enterprise, just as I claim the right, later on in the program, to define what I mean by private enterprise. I think that there are some areas—in fact, a very large number—which Johnston and I would agree with you are legitimate areas for state enterprise. . . .

MR. LASKI: Thank you.

MR. BENTON: . . . assuming you can put the phrase "state enterprise" together and make it hold together. Johnston, we certainly do not question the role of the state in war. We do not question the role of the state in peacetime over the armed forces, or the post office, or the lighthouses. . . .

MR. JOHNSTON: . . . or perhaps education or perhaps social security or reforestation or soil conservation, obviously.

MR. LASKI: What about natural monopolies, Johnston?

MR. JOHNSTON: Natural monopolies can be operated better, in my opinion, under private enterprise with government regulation than they can under government ownership. You know that to be true. As an illustration, your telephone system right here in England where we are sitting here tonight is owned by the government. Our telephone system in America is owned privately and regulated by the government. I think that you will agree with me that the telephone system is operated more efficiently in the United States by far than it is here in England.

MR. BENTON: The area of natural monopoly, Johnston, is one in which men who, in general, will agree with you and me might disagree—a good many of them—on the role of the state. I know some who would favor more government regulation or even government ownership.

MR. LASKI: At any rate we are all three agreed that, whether the main emphasis is on private enterprise or on public enterprise, under all circumstances there is a considerable area that the state must cultivate on behalf of the community in peacetime and under normal circumstances.

MR. BENTON: Yes, a considerable area. The difference between you and Johnston and me, on the other hand, is just what constitutes that area. That is really the key to our discussion today of the economic system.

MR. LASKI: I accept that.

MR. BENTON: I would like to ask you, Laski, assuming that you are in a position of authority in this country—say, you are the Prime Minister—just what you would do in applying the principles you have been advocating to the economy in England and, of course, by inference, to the economy in America.

MR. LASKI: May I begin by saying first of all, quite decisively, that I am a democrat, and, therefore, the supposition must be that my party has been elected to the government of this country by a majority of the people of this country.

MR. BENTON: That is fine.

MR. LASKI: The first things that I should want to do would be to nationalize the banking system; to nationalize the land; to nationalize mines and power and transport. They are the first big bite that I would take off this particular cherry.

MR. JOHNSTON: I would say that that was taking a bite out of the cherry and ruining the whole cherry.

MR. BENTON: Or swallowing it anyway.

MR. JOHNSTON: If you Socialists are really on the level and mean business, why don't you say that you are going to swallow the whole cherry?

MR. LASKI: My poor dear Johnston, because we are social democrats and not revolutionary communists. We are thinking in terms of the piecemeal consummation of the economic system. That is the essential difference (and if you stay here long enough, you will learn it) between the philosophy of the Labour party and the philosophy of the Communist party.

MR. JOHNSTON: I claim that that would deaden freedom of initiative. You would then have a static society with everyone in a groove, with no opportunity for advancement and promotion.

MR. BENTON: Laski's social democrats propose substituting a group of state monopolies for private monopolies and ultimately aim at one giant monopoly to absorb the economic system. Of course, I personally believe that you cannot get the imagination, inventiveness, or creative drive in any planned central economy that we can get, in America at least, from privately managed enterprises. In America we have two million independent business enterprises employing one or more people; we have another million people who are self-employed and about six million farmers who run their own businesses. This makes a total of nine million independent enterprises. The hope of the American economy, in my opinion, for inventiveness and improvement rests around the imagination of these nine million enterprises, and, of course, the millions of others yet to be born.

MR. LASKI: I think that you have dreamed the wrong dream. Is that what you hope? I doubt its realization. You have a century and a half of American history in which you very rarely attained a high level of employment, except where war has demanded the services of the masses who have been so continuously unemployed throughout your history.

MR. JOHNSTON: You have just been having nightmares. That is all that is wrong with you. I disagree with you. There have been many periods in which we have attained high levels of employment in our country.

MR. BENTON: Dreams or nightmares, I think that Laski wants to amputate the arms of the patient because it has the itch.

MR. JOHNSTON: In other words, Laski, as we would say in America, you want to throw the baby out with the bath water.

MR. LASKI: Now, I have two metaphors on my hands to deal with. So far as your amputation is concerned, may I point out respectfully that the Venus de Milo is the result of the amputation.

MR. JOHNSTON: Yes, but she was a cracked girl, and is that the kind of a girl you like?

MR. LASKI: Well, it would be a better world if every girl looked like the Venus de Milo.

MR. BENTON: I have heard of the Venus de Milo's figure and that her profile is famous, but I still prefer my girls with arms that they can use.

MR. JOHNSTON: Laski, you can show me no place in the world under a system of absolute regimentation where the government has controlled everything where you have materially raised the standard of living or of happiness of the people.

MR. LASKI: Just one moment, Johnston. First of all, your word *regimentation*. That is a colorful word; it is intended and used by you for the purpose of importing prejudice into this argument.

MR. JOHNSTON: Not at all, Laski, not any more than the word *monopoly* may be used for importing prejudice.

MR. LASKI: Johnston, I have not used the word *monopoly* a single time in the course of this talk.

MR. JOHNSTON: I do not know how we have missed it.

MR. BENTON: I do not either.

MR. LASKI: If you compare the progress of the Soviet Union since 1919 with the progress either of the United States or of Great

Britain since 1919, the advantage in employment and in happiness is all on the side of the Soviet Union.

MR. BENTON: Even if you are right, the baby in the bath, which was the Soviet Union in 1918, did not have any way to grow but up. It is a very different thing to judge the growth of the illiterate child into school age and then on into grammar school than it is the development of countries such as our own, England and the United States.

Merely because the Soviet Union has made progress, and, of course, it has made remarkable progress in the economic sphere, and at immense sacrifice, it does not follow that similar methods would or should be applied to the economic systems of our own countries.

MR. JOHNSTON: Benton, you know that you have heard me say before that we in America have nothing but praise for the magnificent fight which the Russian people have made in this way. In America we have always admired the people of Russia, but we know that the introduction of their political and economic system into the United States would not raise the standard of living of our people, and that is what I am interested in.

MR. BENTON: Let us see just where we are. We seem to have agreed that the achievement of high levels of employment and production is a major economic problem of our time. We certainly disagree on the method of attacking this problem. Laski looks at it as a Socialist. Johnston and I look at it with a continuing faith in the unfolding and future development of the American system.

I think that we should try to define more clearly, Johnston, what we mean by a private enterprise system. You have indicated in what you have said and in what you have written, as president of the United States Chamber of Commerce, that you are looking toward a development of the enterprise system after the war and not merely a return to the good old days of 1929.

MR. JOHNSTON: Obviously not. We have learned a great deal during this depression and during the war. We have unlearned a lot, too. What we should do is to stimulate the individual to the fullest possible extent to make use of the advantages and talents which he may have. The individual must have opportunity as well as security. Security is necessary, but it is a dull thing. You can have security in a jail. Opportunity is the real hope and the real inspiration. In America I want to preserve the chance to take a chance.

MR. LASKI: Johnston, that is a superb phrase. It is pure rhetoric. I am interested, as I want you to be interested, in the sharecropper of Arizona, in the pecan sheller in San Antonio, and in the fruitpicker in the Imperial Valley.

MR. JOHNSTON: We are interested in him.

MR. LASKI: I want to know how, in America, you are going, first of all, to lift the shadows of fear from off their lives and then, secondly, because they are no longer afraid, give them the opportunities you talk about so eloquently.

MR. BENTON: Wait a second, there is no idea on Johnston's or my part to duck that question, but you are posing a vital social as well as an economic problem, and I may tell you that the business-men in America are increasingly conscious of that problem. We know that we cannot have a prospering economic system in the United States unless these questions are solved. But this subject really needs a University of Chicago Round Table to itself.

MR. LASKI: Very well, let me take John Smith, anywhere in the United States—a simple, ordinary man. How are you going to put purchasing power into the hands of John Smith and millions of other men and women like him?

MR. JOHNSTON: That is just exactly what we are going to do. We have that effective demand in the United States today. Effective demand will continue after the war. The rest of the world will also demand goods and services, if this demand is not stifled by the controls which you advocate.

MR. BENTON: I know that you will agree with me, Johnston, that the problem in our country (I will not speak for England) will probably be to control the demand for quite a period after the war.

MR. LASKI: By the state?

MR. BENTON: There is no doubt that we cannot get rid of state controls the day war ends. That would create a great danger, because there will be a hundred billion dollars in purchasing power in private hands in the United States by the end of this year and a great shortage of goods and a great demand for goods. The real issue in the period right after the war is not the achievement of demand but the maintenance of that demand thereafter.

MR. JOHNSTON: You are absolutely right. Quite obviously, at the end of the last war we had a boom period due to the fact that a great amount of consumption goods had not been manufactured in the war period. The maintenance of that demand after the war is going to depend, to a large degree, on the kind of friendly political climate in which the economy has a chance to exist.

MR. BENTON: That's the heart of it.

MR. JOHNSTON: And the stimulation of creative desire on the part of all our people. We have only begun to explore the frontiers of the mind. We have only begun to understand what we can do in the realm of science and of invention and of new products. We have only begun to raise the standard of living of the people of our country. We must divorce ourselves, once and for all, from the withering influence of bureaucrats who would keep our economy on a dead and dull level.

MR. BENTON: I guess that we will have to admit, Johnston, that there are business and labor practices, too, that have had a restrictive effect on both employment and production. The proper political climate, as I define it, at least, involves the removal of every sort of restriction that holds back high levels of production and employment.

MR. LASKI: Benton, I'm profoundly moved. From the way you two talk, an outsider like myself would imagine that every businessman in the United States was an artist, pursuing his business for his own sake. Everybody knows of the restrictive practices of business all over the world, not the least those restrictive practices in the United States.

In a war period, of course, I do not deny that the climate of danger calls out the highest of which most men are capable in the attempt to protect the country to which they belong.   But, when that climate of danger is passed and men have returned to the coldness of what Mr. Harding called "normalcy," I am not so sure that there is evoked from businessmen, then, the kind of answer that the world requires—the dream that Johnston is talking about of scientific progress and the high standard of living.   It is not so easy, then, in a competitive economy.

MR. JOHNSTON: You know that restrictions are being removed constantly.   Business is removing and shedding its restrictions. But what you want to do is to shackle the entire economy with much more rigid restrictions imposed by government.   The possibility that they cannot be removed to permit free enterprise to function, I believe, is simply the counsel of despair.

MR. BENTON: If I agreed with Laski that there was no possibility of removing the restrictions, I think I would have to agree with him that I would prefer government control, through representatives of the people, to control in private hands.

The basic problem in America of restoring private risk-taking involves the stimulation of competition between firms and individuals.

MR. JOHNSTON: I want the same opportunity for the young man that I had after the last war—the freedom to choose for himself and not to have that choice made by some bureaucrat; the freedom to invest his money as he chooses and not to have that money taken away by taxation because the bureaucrat knows better how to invest it than he does.

MR. BENTON: Good!

MR. LASKI: It is marvelous—in a perspiration of passionate excitement Johnston has rediscovered Woodrow Wilson's New Freedom, which dates from 1913.

MR. JOHNSTON: Yes, and my ideal has been unchanged throughout the ages.   It was not Woodrow Wilson who discovered it; it has been the ideal of man since he crawled out of savagery into civilization.   It has been the ideal for thousands of years, and you know it.

MR. BENTON: That brings us to the conclusion of our broadcast today—the first broadcast of the University of Chicago Round Table ever held outside the United States.

We have agreed that the core of the problem of the economic system is securing high levels of employment and production. That is the imperative need.

We disagree radically on how to solve this problem. Laski takes the viewpoint that state ownership and control of business and enterprise are essential to the achievement of high levels of production and employment. Johnston and I, on our part, take the view that high levels of employment and production can best be achieved through the initiative, enterprise, and imagination of millions of individuals, operating in a political climate favorable to the exercise of their enterprise.

Johnston and I favor competitive capitalism which calls for the maximum use of private enterprise. Laski, for his part, favors the maximum use of government enterprise.

CHAPTER X

Improving Your Diction

You may be one of those fortunate few whose language is wholly satisfactory to the public ear. You may speak all your words with an easy, unaffected distinctness and a precision that is pleasing to the listener. If that is the case, you were no doubt brought up in a remarkably favorable speech environment and have had discipline in correct articulation of speech sounds.

The fact is, we are, as is often said, a nation of mumblers. We don't open our mouths enough, we make a hash of vowels and consonants, we drop syllables, and we run words together in a lazy, slipshod indifference. We seem to have a democratic contempt for the style and art that have made civilized speech so different from the grunts of savages. Many who know better will adopt the worst crudities so as not to appear snobbish. The college boy would rather sound like a tough guy than like a sissy.

The radio, however, is really doing something to this attitude. It is one thing to see a person talk and quite another only to hear him. A pleasant smile, kind eyes, an alert and interested manner will often get us to excuse, to overlook, seriously faulty diction. The radio voice comes into the home alone. It is not escorted by protecting and compensating factors of personality. There is nothing to suggest, "I am really a pretty nice person. I hope you won't mind my tossing the language around a bit carelessly."

We are listening with more awareness and becoming more conscious of articulation, pronunciation, timing, and inflection. Radio speakers are improving and, because they have a much greater public, are doing more to better popular diction than the fine actors whose tradition and responsibility it has been to serve as models of agreeable, cultivated speech.

Anybody who is not handicapped by defective speech organs can easily make all the sounds of the English language. Foreign accent need not worry the occasional speaker, provided he knows our grammar and speaks our language with care. The fact is that the foreigner usually speaks English words with much greater respect than the rest of us and charms us with his somewhat overprecise enunciation. We are often in a worse state of sinning than he because we are the victims of bad habits, and habit, as the Russians say, is a shirt we wear till death.

There is only one cure for a bad habit, and that is an incentive strong enough to keep us practicing and drilling for a new and better habit. The teacher of English corrects his own faulty speech habits because he can't get jobs unless the principals and superintendents think he is a good model for students. The business executive who meets cultivated persons knows he will lose business unless he sounds reasonably educated in speech. The public speaker soon is painfully aware of the necessity for clear, accurate, effortless enunciation. Everybody improves with the persistent stimulus of profit, prestige, or promotion.

Suppose you wanted to be a radio announcer. You would be handed a sheet of paper and told to read aloud this list of words. They look easy enough. What's the trick? Anyone can pronounce

America	what	modern
government	always	united
liberty	athletic	understand
program	film	Arctic
just	New England	battle
really	Saturday	Catholic
duty	today	regular
amateur	tobacco	particular
because	gentlemen	accurate

Any high-school boy ought to get 100 per cent on that test, but it's 100 to 1 that he won't even pass. Out of a class of fifty several will get zero. That's the measure of the lack of attention given in America to the mother tongue.

Here is how these words are maltreated every day, and, common as they are, it is no great wonder if the average reader makes a complete failure of them: *Amarica, guv'mint, libidy, program, jis', reely, doody, amacher, becuz, wut, ahlwiz, athuletic, fillum, Noo Englan', Sad'y, tuhday, tuhbaccuh, gen'l-m'n, mawd'n, unided, unnerstan', Artic, baddle, Cath'lic, reg'lar, partickeler, ackerate.*

Lack of sensitive hearing and lack of care are behind all this. Take the word *duty.* It will stand for a large group. We don't say *moosic* for *music,* or *boogle* for *bugle.* Why do we say *dooty, noos, noospaper, Toosday, stoopid, dook,* etc.? Simply because it is a little harder to make the *you* sound after *d, m, s,* and *t* than after *m* or *b.* Listen to radio announcers and notice how careful they are with this long *u.* You may have to practice to make your tongue more darting and flexible. To get the *y* sound press the tip of the tongue firmly against the hard palate, just above the teeth, and draw it away promptly as you go into the *u.* Sluggish tongue, lips, and jaw are responsible for all the indistinctness and inaccuracy. In words like *elm, film, athletics*, it is the failure to keep the tongue firmly in place after *l* and *th* which allows the extra syllable to be sounded.

So with words like *united, democratic, battle*. The tongue should move with vigor, and not give a soft *d* for a hard *t*. People just won't finish the job. Where the languid *d* will serve, as in *understand*, they drop the whole idea and give us the sloppy *unnerstan'*.

The word *just* means *exact, accurate*. Why not give the word its long overdue justice and stop calling it *jis'* or *jes'?* There's more to it than mere articulation. You feel that a person so heedless and unobserving in such a simple matter of good manners is bound to be unreliable and unintelligent in more important things.

There isn't much need to discuss this phase of diction. You know how syllables are left out in such barbarisms as *lib'ry, fact'ry, m'not'nous, di'mond, reelize, batt'ry*. It's too bad more persons don't recognize the *g* in *recognize*, and of course we have to give up altogether with words like *kept, fifths, costs, insists, brand-new*, and anything that begins with *wh*. They are too much work for mealy mouths.

Wh is a fundamental sound in our language, yet three quarters of the population neglects it. Say, "Walt Whitman." Are you sounding the *h?* Many persons have so neglected this sound effect that they can't produce it. It's the spelling that troubles them. It ought to be *hw* in words like *what, which, where, when, white, wharf*. Say *hoo-wen*. Then shrink the first syllable and say *h'wen*. If the word were spelled *hwen* it would be easy.

You get the general meaning of this brief lecture. If we were half as dull and tired a race as our enunciation would imply, we would be easy marks for any part of the Axis. We simply have not been interested enough to pay attention to accuracy, neatness, and grace in diction.

Besides listening and studying differences in speech sounds, you may have to be more aware of your tongue. "Speak the speech," said Hamlet, "trippingly on the tongue; but if you mouth it, as many of your players do, I had as lief the town-crier spoke my lines." That word *trippingly* connotes all that Alexander Melville Bell, centuries later, set us as the standard of good diction:

Words should issue from the mouth as coins newly issued from the mint, deeply and accurately impressed, perfectly finished, neatly struck by the proper organs, sharp, distinct, in due succession and of due weight.

Tongue, lips, and jaw may need special exercise; and the teeth may need attention. Teachers often recommend that the tongue be stuck out as far as possible, moved from side to side, curled up inside the mouth toward the back, brought forward again, the tip darting from one point to another on the hard palate. If the tongue isn't nimble and sure, the articulation will not be sharp and distinct.

But to make words "deeply and accurately impressed" and "of due weight" the jaw and the lips must take active part. They are frequently stiff and inflexible and responsible for the mouthing Shakespeare complained of. No matter how loud the voice may sound, the unresponsive lips and jaw befog the language.

That rusty jaw needs plenty of exercise. It is the cause of mumbling. Say, *ah!* and open your mouth wide. Place the first two fingers, one above the other, in your mouth while you are saying *ah*, just to be sure that your mouth is wide open. Continue with *foh fah!*, testing with your fingers, occasionally, on *fah!* To stretch the mouth and loosen the jaw, yawn a good deal. You can yawn at any time by opening the mouth as far as possible and holding the position until the yawn breaks.

The jaw should move up and down for the several vowels. Look into the mirror and say, *ah, a, e, i, o, u.* Exaggerate a bit, keeping the jaw active. Most persons sound as though the jaw were clamped and as though they were stingily trying to push all words through a narrow slit between the teeth. Drill on the broad *a*'s until you get the habit of dropping the jaw loosely. Repeat this list frequently: *alms, arm, harm, barn, calm, palm, qualm, lark, hark, stark.*

In connection with the long vowels and some of the consonants we have to consider the element of time. Speakers don't linger long enough on certain letters to make the words distinctly. Practice these two lines from Tennyson:

> Sunset and evening star,
> And one clear call for me!

Hold the *n* in *sunset* and the *ng* in *evening*. Make the *d* in *and* audible, hold the *n* in *one* and the *ll* in *call*. Say *for*, not *fer*.

Give special attention to *l*'s and *d*'s in the following list, but don't say *golduh, colduh,* etc. *Gold, cold, sold, doled, old, bold, rolled, told, mold, fold, wold, hold.*

Pronounce the final consonants distinctly in words like these:

> bean, dean, clean, green, deem, gleam, ream, seem.
> accept, kept, crept, slept, wept, tripped, stepped.
> costs, exists, guests, insists, tastes, crafts.
> depths, fifths, twelfths, gifts, lifts, width, sixth.

Take your time on the following doggerel and carve every word out neatly:

> Amidst the mists and coldest frosts,
> With stoutest wrists and loudest boasts,
> He hits his fists against the posts,
> And still insists he sees the ghosts.

You still need two or three exercises for the lips. The upper lip often seems rigid, immovable. Say, *oo-aw-ee*. Notice how the lips are rounded on *oo* and stretched on *ee*. Purse your lips for a whistle and then say, *whistle, whisper, whip, wharf, what, white.* Be sure to sound the *h*'s. Stretch the upper lip frequently by extending it outward until it touches the nose. Jaws and lips can get coordinated exercise on *yah-hoo, yah-hoo, yah-hoo; me-ow-oo, me-ow-oo, me-ow-oo.* Read these sentences aloud carefully:

We wondered why we should worry as we wound our wintry way.

What white wharf would welcome the white whale?

Bring a bit of buttered brown bran bread.

Peter Piper picked a peck of pickled peppers.

Boldly by battery besiege Belgrade.

Men march 'midst mounds, motes, mountains, murderous mines.

You have become conscious of the traps in words and, one at a time, you haven't any real difficulty in mastering them. When on your guard you can speak these common words confidently and correctly. But your real test is still to come. How good are you when you combine words into phrases and sentences? Do they still come trippingly on the tongue, neatly struck, in due succession and of due weight? Do you speak with the easy correctness of good manners, or is your speech labored and self-conscious? Do you lapse into vulgarisms that may be condoned by your acquaintances but that will never do on the air?

We are all afflicted, at times, with a little crumbling or sleaziness in speech. Indeed, our speech would be too formal and artificial if it were pronounced just as it is printed. Good sense and good taste allow for considerable shrinkage. Diction is a matter of etiquette, a way of articulation that is agreeable to the majority of reasonably educated people, and they would be as much annoyed by overpreciseness as by thoughtless crudities.

In beginning a speech it is correct to say "Ladies 'n gentlemen!" He works for his "bread 'n butter," is right, but "Bread and butter are on the table" requires a different spread. *Raspberry*, *cupboard*, and *forehead* are pronounced in a way you couldn't guess from the spelling.

We used to hear an announcer who for months amused us by the way he read the baseball scores. He would say, "No hits, no runs, no erroars." He wanted to give each syllable its "due weight," but he apparently didn't know baseball. It's more likely that he thought the fans were just a bit careless in calling the word *errers*. He would show his public that a careful announcer would not shrink that *o* into *e*. He had never heard anybody say *erroar*, but he would stick to the spelling—a reckless policy with the English language. *Actor*, *governor*, *doctor*—practically all nouns ending in *or*—are pronounced as though they ended in *er*. Consult your dictionary when in doubt.

As for vulgarisms, the "gotta's," the "gonna's," and the "gimme's" are the commonest offenders. But almost every sentence may produce mortification for the untrained speaker. Take the apparently harmless sentence: "What did you say to the fellow in the wheel chair?" It is very likely to sound like this, "Wudjuh say't the feller in the weel chair?" Here is another passage: "I've got to go now. I want to hear his lecture on Old English." Its common rendering is: "I gotta go now. I wanna hear 'is lecture on Ole English." "What do you think of that?" becomes "Wudduh yuh thinkuh that?" "Get some ice cream for us" is popularly given as "Git sommice cream f'rus."

There isn't much profit in discussing the technicalities of every consonant and vowel and warning you of the atrocities that speakers so callously inflict upon them. The illustrations we have given will serve to remind you that a little care and thought about these matters can greatly improve the quality of your diction. Besides, you have to learn your language by ear, not by print.

Four suggestions are practical. First, speak at a slower rate, noting words more deliberately. "Take care of the consonants," Aubrey Smith used to advise youngsters in show business, "and the vowels will take care of themselves." That's a good rough-and-ready rule, but you have time to study and shape the vowels for more fullness and resonance.

Second, read aloud as much as you can. Ask a member of the family to sit by with pencil and paper and take notes of questionable articulation and pronunciation. Get used to some of the radio limitations. Have him sit to one side or behind you, or better still, put a screen between you. If he doesn't see your face while you are reading he will form a better objective judgment, and you, if you don't see him writing, will not be disturbed by his listing your errors. Read prose for improving distinctness and accuracy, and poetry for better tone.

Third, sit before the radio frequently and study the diction of announcers, well-known personages, and occasional speakers. Try to discover the specific things that make their enunciation agreeable or disagreeable. Remember that good use does not require uniformity or regimentation. Each large section of the English-speaking world is a law unto itself. East and West, North and South have different accents, somewhat different rhythms and idioms, and the speakers should be judged by the prevailing good use of their own region. The violations we have been concerned with are, however, equally disagreeable to all discriminating listeners.

Fourth, listen everywhere and be aware! Develop the artistic spirit toward sound. Associate with skilled speakers. You will absorb their easy and comfortable assurance with correct manners in diction. Don't, just to be a regular guy, go all out for the sloppy indifference of some of your acquaintances. After all, you're in training and you can't break faith with your public. In mental, spiritual, and vocal discipline we need more of the ascetic rigor of the athlete.

We are concluding this chapter with passages selected to keep you alert with ideas, vocabulary, and enunciation. Study them carefully for the central thoughts and the subordinate details. Get familiar enough with them so that you enjoy them. Don't read them aloud until you are like the salesman who "knows his stuff" and is eager to display it. If there are lines you don't understand or rich details you are insensitive to, your reading aloud will disclose that fact through dull inflection and poor timing. Be a conductor who delights to interpret the eloquence and beauty of a great composer.

The second objection of materialism to the existence of an immaterial soul is that the condition of the body affects the soul, inevitably and always. A little improper food taken into the system affects the mind; a drop of blood extravasated in the brain destroys the power of thought; as the body grows old, the mind weakens; as the brain-fibres decay, memory goes; without phosphorus, no thought—is not then thought the result of the body? To this, however, the answer is conclusive. All these facts only prove that while the soul is in this body, the body is its necessary organ of communication with the outward world. Just as a carpenter cannot work when his tools are dull; as the most accomplished musician cannot charm our souls when the strings of his piano are out of tune, or broken; so the soul cannot communicate with us when the body is disordered. It is highly probable that we could not think if the proper amount of phosphorus were not supplied to the brain. But this is not such a great discovery. Not "phosphorus" alone, but a good many other chemical elements have always been known to be necessary. Without oxygen, no thought; without hydrogen and carbon, no thought. All this merely means that while the soul remains in its present environment, it needs a healthy bodily organization with which to do its work.

JAMES FREEMAN CLARKE.

Let us look back three or four centuries. Then, as now, the great mass of mankind were governed by the three main wishes: the wish for vigor of body, including the absence of painful feelings; for wealth, or the power of procuring the external conditions of bodily enjoyment—these during life; and security from pain and continuance of happiness hereafter. Then, as now, men were desirous to attain them by some easier means than those of temperance, industry, and strict justice. They gladly therefore applied to the Priest, who could ensure them happiness hereafter without the performance of their duties here; to the Lawyer, who could make money a substitute for a right cause; to the Physician, whose medicines promised to take the sting out of the tail of their sensual indulgences, and let them fondle and play with vice, as with a charmed serpent; to the Alchemist, whose gold-tincture would enrich them without toil or economy; and to the Astrologer, from whom they could purchase foresight without knowledge or reflection.

SAMUEL TAYLOR COLERIDGE.

There is a great fact known to us more certainly than the existence of matter: it is the unity of consciousness. I know that I exist, and that I am One. Hermann Lotze's supreme argument against materialism is the unity of consciousness. I know that I am *I*, and not *you;* and I know *this* to my very finger-tips. That finger is part of my organism, not of yours. To the last extremity of every nerve, I know that I am One. The unity of consciousness is a fact known to us by much better evidence than the existence of matter. I am a natural realist in philosophy, if I may use a technical term: I believe in the existence of both matter and mind. There are two things in the universe; but I know the existence of mind better than I know the existence of matter. Sometimes in dreams we fall down precipices and awake, and find that the gnarled savage rocks had no existence. But we touched them; we felt them; we were bruised by them. Who knows but that some day we may wake, and find that all matter is merely a dream: Even if we do that, it will yet remain true that I am *I*. There is more support for idealism than for materialism; but there is no sufficient support for either. If we are to reverence all, and not merely a fraction, of the list of axiomatic or self-evident truths, if we are not to play fast and loose with the intuitions which are the external tests of verity, we shall believe in the existence of both matter and mind. Hermann Lotze holds that the unity of consciousness is a fact absolutely incontrovertible and absolutely inexplicable on the theory that our bodies are woven by a complex of physical arrangements and physical forces, having no co-ordinating presiding power over them all. I know that there is a co-ordinating presiding power somewhere in me. I am *I*. I am One. Whence the sense of a unity of consciousness, if we are made up according to Spencer's idea, or Huxley's, of infinitely multiplex molecular mechanisms? We have the idea of a presiding power that makes each man one individuality from top to toe. How do we get it? It must have a sufficient cause. To this hour, no man has explained the unity of consciousness in consistency with the mechanical theory of life.

JOSEPH COOK.

Great princes have great playthings.   Some have play
At hewing mountains into men, and some
At building human wonders mountain high.
Some have amused the dull sad years of life,
Life spent in indolence, and therefore sad,
With schemes of monumental fame; and sought
By pyramids and mausolean pomp,
Short-lived themselves, to immortalize their bones.
Some seek diversion in the tented field,
And make the sorrows of mankind their sport.
But war's a game, which, were their subjects wise,
Kings would not play at.   Nations would do well
To extort their truncheons from the puny hands
Of heroes, whose infirm and baby minds
Are gratified with mischief, and who spoil
Because men suffer it, their toy, the world.

WILLIAM COWPER.

CHAPTER XI

Words Commonly Mispronounced

English pronunciation is full of traps for the careless or unwary. Even the announcers, the readers of commercials, who, of all people, should be on their guard, make many inexcusable errors. They have dictionaries at hand but they won't take the trouble to look up a word that appears so utterly harmless that it couldn't possibly be muffed.

The spelling of our language is very deceptive. Vowels have many different sounds not indicated by print, and consonants are often unpredictable. You can't be sure whether *g* is *j*; whether *c* is *s* or *k*; whether letters are silent, as in *debt*, *sign*, *victuals*, *mortgage*.

Guessing where the accent falls is still more precarious. Is *acclimate* pronounced "a KLYE mit" or "AK li mayt?" Until recently "a KLYE mit" was the only correct pronunciation but Webster, in the latest edition, allows "AK li mayt."

There is no board of linguists to which these matters may be referred or which has authority to give us the correct pronunciations. The dictionaries are accepted as authorities because they record the common usage of educated persons. This so-called "good use" is not always easy to discover because the usage of cultivated speakers is not uniform or unanimous. And, with respect to many words, fashions change.

Take the word *inquiry*, for instance. Almost everybody nowadays pronounces it "IN kwi ri"—a decisive accent on the first syllable and a short, obscure, fading-out *i* in the second and third syllables. But elderly persons know that it wasn't so many years ago when practically everyone said "in KWYE ri," and that is still the preferred form in *Webster's Dictionary*. So the dictionaries frequently find it necessary to record two, and sometimes three, acceptable pronunciations for certain words. In such cases use the pronunciation most common in your section of the country.

Don't let this latitude tempt you, however, to think that the way you pronounce a word is in such general use that reference to the dictionary is not necessary. In Boston you may hear two-thirds of the population mispronounce *municipal*. They are likely to call it "myu ni SIP al" instead of "myu NIS i pal." The word *theater* gets similar abuse. There is no authority for "the AY ter," but it persists as a popular error. On the air such mistakes are costly. They are at once detected and reported. And with what glee! You'd think the speaker had committed a major crime against society.

One thing more needs to be said. Actually few persons know how to use a dictionary easily and accurately. Ask the average college student to bring his dictionary to class and read from it—and with all the evidence before him he will still make a hash of the word. If he has taken the trouble to look at the bottom of the page and be guided by the simple diacritical marks and illustrative words, he still mispronounces. He doesn't notice over which syllable the accent mark is placed or whether the accented vowel is long or short. He sounds like a dunce because he hasn't asked himself what is liable to be tricky about the word.

Consider the word *vagary*. Offhand the student might call it "VAG a ri." But surprises in other words should warn him that there are several possibilities here. The *a* in *vag* may be long, as in *vague*. If he thinks of that, he may still take it for granted that the accent is on the first syllable and not observe that the accent is on the second. Even when that somewhat startling fact is pointed out to him he has by now such a fixation for "VAG a ri" or "VAGUE a ri" that he just cannot say "va GAIR i" until the instructor has pronounced it for him once or twice.

When a vowel is not accented it has a tendency to become thin and muffled—"obscure," the dictionaries call it. With the accent on the second syllable, the first *a* in *vagary* becomes practically negligible. It is neither long nor short. You can't tell by the pronunciation whether it is *a, e, i*, or *u*. It is like the *a* in *senate* or *sofa*.

The dictionary is a fascinating book. Its derivations and word histories as well as its definitions, synonyms, antonyms, and pronunciations open up many avenues of interesting and productive exploration. No one who aspires to a mature and richly expressive vocabulary can afford to neglect this great storehouse of information.

Getting back to pronunciation, practice with the dictionary will help you to acquire a confident and flexible utterance. It will keep you aware of snags and give you an easy skill in adjusting teeth, tongue, and lips to unexpected combinations. Think of the number of persons who have trouble in making the shift from "hos PIT a b'l" (wrong) to "HOS pi ta b'l" (right); from "des PIK a b'l" (wrong) to "DES pi ka b'l" (right); from "a PLIK a b'l" (wrong) to "AP li ka b'l" (right); from "in ex PLIK a b'l" (wrong) to "in EX pli ka b'l" (right); from "fawr MID a b'l" (wrong) to "FAWR mi da b'l" (right).

The words listed below have given plenty of trouble. They are common words that can't be readily avoided.

It is only prudence to study them carefully and correct any misconceptions you may have about them. The simplified phonetic spelling noted above is used below. Accented syllables are emphasized by capitals in the hope that you will stress them vigorously.

accompanist (a KUM pa nist, *not* a KUM pa nee ist)

acoustics (a KOOS tiks *or* a COWS tiks)

acumen (a KYU men, *not* AK yu men)

adept (AD ept *or* a DEPT)

adieu (a DYU *or* a DYUR)

admiralty (AD mir al ti, *not* ad MYE ral ti)

adobe (a DOH bi)

adult (a DULT)

adversary (AD ver ser i, *not* ad VERS e ri)

agenda (a JEN da)

aggrandizement (a GRAN diz ment, *not* a gran DIZE ment)

agile (AJ il *or* AJ ile)

ague (AY gyu)

alias (AY li as, *not* a LYE as)

alma mater (AL ma MAY ter *or* AL ma MAH ter)

amateur (am a TER *or* AM a tyur)

amenable (a MEE na b'l *or* a MEN a b'l)

anchovy (an CHOH vi *or* AN choh vi)

applicable (AP li ka b'l, *not* a PLIK a b'l)

archangel (ARK AYN jel)

archdeacon (ARCH DEE c'n)

archipelago (ar ki PEL a goh)

architect (AR ki tekt)

aspirant (as PIRE ant *or* AS pi rant)

autopsy (AW top si)

aviator (AY vi ay ter)

awry (a RYE, *not* AW ri)

bade (bad)

bestial (BEST yal, *not* BEEST yal)

betrothed (be TROTHT *or* be TROHTHD)

biography (bye OG ra fi)

blasé (blah ZAY *or* BLAH zay)

blatant (BLAY tant)

bona fide (BOH na FYE dee)

bouquet (boo KAY *or* boh KAY)

bourgeois (boor ZHWAH *or* BOOR zhwah)

braggadocio (brag a DOH shi oh)

bravado (bra VAH doh)

bronchial (BRONG ki al, *not* BRON i kal)

brooch (brooch *or* brohch)

brusque (brusk *or* broosk—*oo* as in *brook*)

buccaneer (buck a NEER)

bulwark (BULL work)

bureaucracy (byu ROK ra si *or* byu ROHK ra si)

cabal (ka BAL, *as in* Al)
cache (kash)
cadaver (ka DAV er *or*
    ka DAY ver)
Celt (selt *or* kelt)
centenary (SEN te ner i *or*
    sen TEN a ri)
cerebral (SER e bral, *not*
    se REE bral)
chagrin (sha GRIN)
chameleon (ka MEE lee un *or*
    ka MEEL yun)
chassis (SHAS ee *or* SHAS is)
chastisement (CHAS tiz ment, *not*
    chas TIZE ment)
chevalier (shev a LEER)
chimera (kye MEE ra *or*
    ki MEE ra)
circuit (SIR kit)
clique (kleek)
column·(KOL um)
comely (KUM li)
comptroller (kon TROHL er)
condolence (kon DOH lens)
conjugal (KON joo gal, *not*
    kon JOO gal)
connoisseur (kon i SIR *or*
    kon i SYUR)
conversant (KON ver sant, *not*
    kon VERS ant)
coupon (KOO pon, *not* KYU pon)
culinary (KYU li ner i)
curator (kyu RAY ter)

data (DAY ta *or* DAH ta)
delegate (DEL e gayt)
derisive (de RYE siv)
despicable (DES pi ka b'l)
deter (de TER)

digitalis (dij i TAY lis)
dilettante (dil e TAN ti)
diocesan (dye OS e san, *not*
    dye o SEE san)
disciplinary (DIS i pli ner i)
dishabille (dis a BEEL)
dishevel (di SHEV'l)
divorcé (di vor SAY)
doughty (DOW ti, *not* DAW ti)
drama (DRAH ma *or* DRAM a)
duce (DOO chay)

eczema (EK ze ma, *not*
    ek ZEEM a)
epitome (e PIT oh mee)
equitable (EK wi ta b'l)
era (EE ra)
err (*er* as in *fern*, not as in *there*)
exquisite (EKS kwi zit, *not*
    eks KWIZ it)
extraordinary
    (eks TROR di ne ri)

façade (fa SAHD)
Fascism (FASH iz'm *or*
    FAS iz'm)
fetish (FEE tish *or* FET ish)
fiancé, *mas.* (fee ahn SAY *or*
    fee AHN say)
fiancée, *fem.* (fee ahn SAY)
finale (fee NAH lee)
finis (FYE nis)
fjord (fyord)
forte, *n.* (fort)
forte, *adj.* (FOR tay)
frailty (FRAYL ti, *not* FRAY al ti
    or FRAY la ti)
fungi (FUN jye)

gala (GAY la *or* GAH la)

gaseous (GAS e us, *not* GASH us)

gauge (gayj)

genuine (JEN yu in, *not* JEN yu wine)

ghoul (gool)

gigantean (jye gan TEE an)

granary (GRAN a ri, *not* GRAIN a ri)

gratis (GRAY tis)

grievous (GREEV us, *not* GREEV e us)

grimace (gri MACE, *not* GRIM us)

habitué (ha bit yu AY *or* ha BIT yu ay)

halibut (HAL i but *or* HOL i but)

hearth (harth)

heinous (HAY nus)

horizon (hoh RYE z'n)

hospitable (HOS pi ta b'l, *not* hos PIT a b'l)

imagery (IM ij ri)

imbroglio (im BROHL yoh)

impetigo (im pe TYE goh)

impious (IM pi us, *not* im PYE us)

impotent (IM poh tent, *not* im POH tent)

incognito (in KOG ni toh, *not* in kog NEE toh)

incomparable (in KOM pa ra b'l)

indefatigable (in dee FAT i ga b'l)

indictment (in DITE ment)

inexorable (in EK soh ra b'l)

infamous (IN fa mus)

inquiry (in KWIRE i *or* IN kwi ri)

irreparable (i REP a ra b'l)

irrevocable (i REV a ka b'l)

khaki (KAH ki, *not* KAK i)

kilometer (KIL oh mee ter, *not* ki LOM e ter)

larynx (LAR ingks, *not* LAR nix)

livelong (LIV long, *not* LIVE long)

longevity (lon JEV i ti, *not* long GEV i ti)

magi (MAY jye, *not* MAG i *or* MAJ i)

maintenance (MAYN te nance, *not* mayn TAY nance)

maniacal (ma NYE a kal)

mauve (mohv, *not* mawv)

memoir (MEM wor)

menu (MEN yu)

messieurs (MES erz *or* MES yerz)

mischievous (MIS chi vus, *not* mis CHEEV i us)

municipal (myu NIS i pal)

naïve (nah EEV)

necromancer (NEK roh man ser)

noblesse oblige (noh BLES oh BLEEZH)

nonpareil (non pa REL)

oasis (oh AY sis *or* OH a sis)

often (OF'n)

oleomargarine (oh le oh MAHR ja reen, *or* MAHR ga reen)

omnipotent (om NIP oh tent, *not* om ni POH tent)

oral (OH ral, *not* OR al)
orgies (OR jiz)
oust (owst, *not* oost)

pachyderm (PAK i derm)
padrone (pah DROH nay)
par excellence (pahr EK se lahns)
parliament (PAHR li ment)
pathos (PAY thos)
patriotic (pay tri OT ik)
penalize (PEE nal ize)
plagiarism (PLAY ji a riz'm)
plague (playg, *not* pleg)
plebeian (ple BEE yan)
plebiscite (PLEB i site *or*
    PLEB i sit)
poignant (POIN yant *or*
    POIN ant)
posse (POS ee)
posthumous (POS tyu mus)
precedence (pre SEED ens)
precedent (PRES e dent)
preferable (PREF er a b'l)
premier (PREE mi er *or*
    pre MEER)
prestige (pres TEEZH *or*
    PRES tij)
preventive (pre VEN tiv, *not*
    pre VEN ta tiv)
primarily (PRIME er il i, *not*
    prye MAIR i li)
pronunciation (proh nun si AY
    shun), *note spelling*
pumpkin (PUMP kin)

quadrupedal (kwod ROO pe dal)
quay (kee)
quietus (kwye EE tus)

rabies (RAY bi eez *or* RAY beez)
ration (RAY shun *or* RASH un)
recipe (RES i pee)
remediable (re MEE di a b'l)
respite (RES pit)
restaurant (RES tu rant, *not*
    ahnt)
revocable (REV oh ka b'l)
robot (ROH bot *or* ROB ot, *not*
    ROH boh)
romance (ro MANS)
route, way, road (root)
route, defeat (rout, *ou* as in *loud*)

sacrifice (SAK ri fise, *i* as in *ice*)
sacrilegious (sak ri LEE jus)
sang-froid (sahng FRWA)
satiety (sa TYE e ti)
scallop (SKOL up *or* SKAL up)
schism (siz'm)
secretive (see KREE tiv, *not*
    SEE kre tiv)
seismic (SIZE mik *or* SISE mik)
semester (se MES ter)
sepulcher (SEP ul ker)
sepulchral (se PUL kral)
sesame (SES a mee)
sinew (SIN yu)
solace (SOL is)
spontaneity (spon ta NEE i ti)
squalor (SKWOL er)
status (STAY tus)
strategic (stra TEE jik)
syringe (SIR inj)

tarpaulin (tahr PAW lin)
theater (THEE a ter, *not* the ET er
    or the AYT er)

traverse (TRAV ers, *not*
  tra VERS)
tribunal (trye BYU nal)
tribune (TRIB yun)

ultimatum (ul ti MAY tum)
usurp (yu ZURP)

vagary (va GAIR i)
valet (VAL et *or* VAL it)
vaudeville (VOHD vil)

vehement (VEE e ment)
victuals (VIT'lz)
virago (vi RAY goh)
vox populi (voks POP yu lye)

xylophone (ZYE loh fohn)

zealot (ZEL ut)
zoology (zoh OL oh ji)
zwieback (TSVEE bahk *or*
  TSWEE bahk)

NAMES OF PLACES FREQUENTLY MISPRONOUNCED

Addis Ababa (AH dis AH ba ba)
Aegean Sea (ee JEE an)
Albuquerque (al byu KER kee)
Aleutian Islands (a LOO shan)
Antarctic (ant AHRK tik)
Antipodes (an TIP oh deez)
Arkansas (AHR kan saw)

Boise (BOI si)
Buenos Aires
  (BWAY nohs EYE rays *or*
  BOH nos AIR ez)

Cádiz (KAY diz)
Copenhagen (kohp'n HAY gen)

Erin (AIR in *or* EER in)

Hawaii (hah WYE ee, *not*
  ha WAH ee)

Jungfrau (YOONG frow)

Lourdes (loord)

Miami (mye AM i)
Mojave (moh HAHV ay)
Moscow (MOS koh, *not*
  MOS cow)

Nice (nees)

Oahu (oh AH hoo)
Osaka (OH sa ka)

Pago Pago (PAHNG oh
  PAHNG oh)
Port Said (sah EED)
Prague (prayg)

Rainier (ray NEER)
Rheims (reemz)
Rio de Janeiro (REE oh day
  zha NAY roh)
Riviera (re VYAIR rah)

Salonika (sah loh NEE ka)
San Joaquin (san wah KEEN)
San Jose (san hoh SAY *or*
  san hoh ZAY)

San Juan (san HWAHN)
Shamokin (sha MOH kin)
Shantung (shahn DOONG)
Smolensk (smo LYENSK)
Stalingrad (sta len GRAHD)

Terre Haute (ter e HOHT)
Tientsin (TIN TSIN)

Vladivostok (vla di vos TAWK)

Wilkes-Barre (WILKS bar i)

NAMES OF PERSONS FREQUENTLY MISPRONOUNCED

Abruzzi (ah BROOT see)
Adonis (a DOH nis)
Aeschines (ES ki neez)
Agassiz (AG a see)
Archimedes (ahr ki MEE deez)

Bagehot (BAJ ut)
Bartholdi (bar tawl DEE)
Boccaccio (bohk KAHT choh)
Boleyn (BOOL in)
Borgia (BAWR jah)

Charlemagne (SHAHR le mayn)
Cheops (KEE ops)
Cibber (SIB er)
Corneille (kawr NAY y')
Cortes (KAWR tez)
Croat (KROH at)

De Valera (day va LAY rah)
Dewar (DYU er)
Diaz (DEE ahz *or* DEE ahth)
Dumas (dyu MAH)
Duse (DOO zay)

Gautama (GAW ta ma)
Genghis Khan (JEN giz KAHN)
Goethals (GOH thalz)

Goethe (GER te)
Grouchy (groo SHEE)

Juárez (HWAH rays)
Jung (yoong)

La Follette (lah FOL et)

Macleod (mak LOWD)
Masaryk (MAH sa reek)
Mascagni (mahs KAHN yee)
Maugham (mawm)
Mercator (mer KAY ter)
Molière (moh LYAIR)
Morgenthau (MAWR gen thaw)
Mussolini (moos soh LEE nee)

Nietzsche (NEE che, final *e* as in *met*)
Nobel (noh BEL)

Penelope (pe NEL oh pee)
Powys (POH is)
Proust (proost)
Ptolemy (TOL e mi)

Richelieu (ree she LYU)
Rodin (roh DANG)
Rostand (raws TAHNG)

Synge (sing)

Taney (TAW ni)
Terpsichore (turp SIK oh ree)
Titian (TISH an)
Toussaint L'Ouverture
   (too SANG   loo ver TYUR)

Vinci, da (dah VEEN chee)

Xanthippe (zan TIP ee)
Xavier (ZAV i er *or* ZAY vi er)

Zoroaster (zoh roh AS ter)
Zuloaga (thoo loh AH gah)

CHAPTER XII

Cultivating the Agreeable Radio Voice

Fortunately we don't all like the same things in voice. Southerners, New Englanders, Westerners prefer their own accents and peculiarities but enjoy the sense of novelty and distinction that accompanies a voice from a distant area. Some voices are agreeable to everybody, others are liked and disliked, and a third group is disagreeable to everyone.

Many speakers sound unlike themselves on the air and experiment a great deal to find a more agreeable pitch level. Some voices are too low. They are dragging "in the mud" and need to be lifted to a level from which they can go down as well as up to get the necessary variety of inflection. Other voices are too high and explosive and come over the air even worse. They must be trained to speak comfortably on a lower level.

Then there are hard voices, metallic voices, nasal voices, gruff voices, all sorts of unpleasant ones. They wouldn't sound so bad if we could see some of the nice faces behind them. These disembodied voices are strangely misleading when we try to guess what sort of persons go with them. Some of the best voices have us making handsome pictures of their possessors. What a shock when we see their photographs for the first time! It all adds to the fun of radio but reminds us how strikingly personality is reduced to voice.

The radio favors the smooth and mellow tone. Imitate the crooner or the "groaner." He operates from a com-

fortable hum out on the lips. He seems to sigh the tone
from the bottom of the lungs and avoids constricting
it in the throat. The tone just floats up on the outgoing
breath.

Get a little conscious of your breathing in speech. It
should be deep enough to expand the diaphragm so that
you will have a good column of air to support the tone that
is made as the breath goes over the vocal cords. There is
nothing difficult about this. Everybody who has to speak
up instinctively inhales deeply to get the necessary volume.
Actors call it "packing the breath against the belt."
You'll get a good tone if you just let go from the lungs
instead of trying to push tone out from the back of the
throat. Most bad tone is caused by this clucking and
squeezing in the throat.

Get used to feeling the outward and inward movements
of the diaphragm. Place your hands, palms in and tips of
fingers touching, just below the sternum, in front, below the
chest, where the ribs meet. Take a deep breath and feel
the diaphragm expand. As you release the breath, say *uh,
uh, uh, uh, uh, uh,* with a relaxed and sighing movement.
Keep the throat relaxed, free from strain or effort.

Now feel the diaphragm acting more vigorously. Take a
deep breath and count ten loudly and boldly, as though you
were directing a class on the gym floor, *one! two! three!*,
etc.

Note the feel of the diaphragm on "Up! Up! Up! from
the bottom of the sea!"

Recite this jingle, which we recall from advertising of the
good old days. Give it heartily and buoyantly. Don't be
afraid to exaggerate and have a little fun with it. It's good
exercise for the diaphragm. Give it a chanting quality.
Take a comfortable deep breath and "give out."

> Ho for the Spotter of Spotless Town,
> He spotted a spot on the butcher's gown,
> 'Twould not be meat for justice' sake
> To roast the butcher at the steak,
> And so behind the bars he'll go!
> Bars of what?   Sapolio!!

You see, the common error of most persons who haven't given thought to proper tone production is to contract the throat. They think of voice as a muscle that has to be worked. It is this tightening and irritating of the throat that gives the tight, hard, metallic quality to tone. Think of the diaphragm as the piston or motor and the lungs as a bellows that closes gradually. Or think of an accordion. You press a stop and take in plenty of air. Then you play the notes as the air is gradually released, and take in air again as you need it.

Relaxation of the throat is hard for some people to manage. It's a matter of the whole body and requires mental and emotional ease. Most of us can achieve a free relaxed tone in private, but the moment we face an audience or the microphone we get tense, tighten up, and spoil those tones which were once full, round, and mellow. Practice and familiarity will bring the necessary release.

To get the habit of the relaxed throat, think the tone forward to the lips. Imagine that you are plucking words off your lips as you might pluck the notes off a banjo or mandolin. Practice with words made out in the front of the mouth, like "Peter Piper picked a peck of pickled peppers" or "The sun rose over the city," or "Dere's a little wheel a-turnin' in my heart." Aim all tone at the upper teeth or hard palate.

The jaw may need loosening exercises. We discussed this in connection with diction. Practice frequently with the exercises on pages 141 and 142.

We spoke earlier in the chapter of the humming exercise. The test of a good voice is the hum that flows as a continuous line through the articulation. It is the resonance, the reverberation that comes from using your mouth, head, and chest as a loud-speaker.

You know how flat some tones are. They seem to be made thinly in the mouth without breath support. They lack sing and vitality. A voice teacher of our acquaintance likes to give out cards to strangers he meets. Under his name are the words, "Teacher of voice," and just below that caption is this free exercise: "Hum and intone more morning songs!" The *m*'s and *n*'s and *ng*'s make the front nasal resonance, and the humming and intoning give you practice in the ring and the chant that are characteristic of the full, free voice. It is the singing speaking voice that you must acquire. No matter how lightly, casually, and informally you talk, that suggestion of a hum should be present. Try these exercises, putting plenty of hum into them:

1. Hummmm!
2. Hummmm! Hummmm! Hummmmm!
3. Hummahh! Hummmee! Hummmoo!
4. Home! Home! Home on the range!
5. Sing a song of sixpence,
   A pocket full of rye;
   Four and twenty blackbirds
   Baked in a pie.
6. I am thy father's spirit;
   Doom'd for a certain term to walk the night,
   And for the day confined to fast in fires,
   Till the foul crimes done in my days of nature
   Are burnt and purged away.

Through better breathing, relaxation, and resonance you will improve the quality of your voice, but quality is said to reflect emotion and mood. In other words, if you are by habit a sympathetic person, something in your voice will reveal that condition. If you are shy, diffident, negative in manner, voice will indicate that, too. If you happen to be chronically grouchy and irritable, which we are sure you are not, your voice will give you away. This is not always so, but it usually is. You've noticed it yourself.

The chief trouble with Americans is that they don't reveal much of anything in voice. They sound dull and lifeless. They don't wear their hearts on their sleeves and they are inclined to suppress sympathetic tones. Much of this is due to self-consciousness that results in flat monotones. They will have to work to recover that natural, spontaneous, bubbling quality that gave color to their voices when they were children.

Consider the actor for a moment; you've got to imitate him. He doesn't, as a rule, know any more about voice, technically, than you have just read. He trains his voice by ear, and you must listen, attentively, too. He knows that it is something in the sound, rather than the word, that moves people. He takes seriously that old story about Nazimova. She was asked at a party, so it goes, to recite something in Russian. She obliged, with something so beautiful, so touching, that everyone was in tears. After the applause one of the ladies recovered enough to ask the actress, "What was that lovely thing? What was it all about?" "That," said Nazimova with an apologetic grin, "that was the Russian alphabet."

The actor spends his life getting and keeping clear, resonant, sympathetic tone. Even when he drinks and smokes too much, he can still hear the tone he wants and make a pretty good stab at it. He has practiced a great variety of expressiveness, the gay, the solemn, the tender, the bold. He has to cultivate audacity, assurance, and flexibility. And so have you, if you want to be at home on the radio. It is a commonplace that the good radio speaker is something of an actor. He has to play his best self, play up to a certain mood or atmosphere, and get the variety and attention that come from skillful timing and inflection.

We'll have more to say about this but we'll close this chapter with more exercises for breathing, relaxation, and resonance. We want you, however, to put even greater thought to reading aloud the passages of different moods, and remember that every sympathetic, gently melancholy, sublime, or hearty tone frees and opens the throat and gives you more resonant quality. But you've got to read with understanding and pleasure. Make it so good that the members of your family will be glad to listen to you.

BREATHING

1. Stand up straight but relaxed with your back against a wall or a door. Press the edge of a book against your stomach to help force out the air as you exhale. Then inhale slowly, noticing the action of the diaphragm. It should push the book away from you. Practice this exercise frequently until you clearly and easily move the book by diaphragmatic breathing.

2. Speak this sentence on one breath: "Uh-uh-uh-utter as many words as you can on one deep breath held back without restraint to voice tone without waste." Until you have practiced a bit you might stop at *breath*. Then, after a while, go as far as *restraint*. Next, with a little speeding up, you can do the whole sentence on a single breath.

3. Read the following passages at a moderate rate of speed, with chant and ring. Notice whether you are breathing deeply and rhythmically enough to avoid a jerky, uneven rate. How

many lines do you speak on a single breath? Be comfortable
and don't strain. Breathe as often as you like.

a. Alone, alone,—all,—all alone;
    Alone on a wide, wide sea.

b. Ring out, wild bells, to the wild sky,
    The flying cloud, the frosty light:
    The year is dying in the night;
    Ring out, wild bells, and let him die.

c. Cannon to right of them,
    Cannon to left of them,
    Cannon behind them
        Volley'd and thunder'd;
    Storm'd at with shot and shell,
    While horse and hero fell,
    They that had fought so well
    Came thro' the jaws of Death,
    Back from the mouth of Hell,
    All that was left of them,
        Left of six hundred.

d. But now farewell. I am going a long way
    With these thou seest—if indeed I go
    (For all my mind is clouded with a doubt)—
    To the island-valley of Avilion;
    Where falls not hail or rain or any snow,
    Nor ever wind blows loudly; but it lies
    Deep-meadowed, happy, fair with orchard lawns
    And bowery hollows crowned with summer sea,
    Where I will heal me of my grievous wound.

4. Here is a paragraph from one of the great orators of the
South, Henry W. Grady. It is from his last speech, generally
considered his best. The speech was delivered at a dinner of
the Boston Chamber of Commerce, December 12, 1889, eleven
days before his death in Atlanta. The selection is especially
good for practice because it has measured, rhythmic cadence.
It should be read with sweeping oratorical intonation. It

encourages deep, sustained, and rhythmical breathing, as well as clear and melodious articulation. Read it slowly.

Far to the South, Mr. President, separated by a line,—once defined in irrepressible difference, once traced in fratricidal blood, and now, thank God, but a vanishing shadow,—lies the fairest and richest domain of this earth. It is the home of a brave and hospitable people. There is centered all that can please or prosper human kind. A perfect climate above a perfect soil yields to the husbandman every product of the temperate zone. There, by night, the cotton whitens beneath the stars, and by day the wheat locks the sunshine in its bearded sheaf. In the same field the clover steals the fragrance of the wind, and tobacco catches the quick aroma of the rains. There are mountains stored with exhaustless treasures; forests vast and primeval, and rivers that, tumbling or loitering, run wanton to the sea. Of the three essential items in all industries,—cotton, iron, and wood,—that region has easy control. In cotton, a fixed monopoly; in iron, proven supremacy; in timber, the reserve supply of the Republic. From this assured and permanent advantage, against which artificial conditions cannot long prevail, has grown an amazing system of industries. Not maintained by human contrivance of tariff or capital, afar off from the fullest and cheapest source of supply, but resting in Divine assurance, within touch of field and mine and forest,—not set amid bleak hills and costly farms from which competition has driven the farmer in despair, but amid cheap and sunny lands, rich with agriculture, to which neither season nor soil has set a limit,—this system of industries is mounting to a splendor that shall dazzle and illumine the world.

That, sir, is the picture and the promise of my home—a land better and fairer than I have told you, and yet but a fit setting, in its material excellence, for the loyal and gentle quality of its citizenship. Against that, sir, we have New England recruiting the Republic from its sturdy loins, shaking from its overcrowded hives new swarms of workers, and touching this land all over with its energy and its courage.

RELAXATION

1. Let your head fall forward limply toward your chest. Open your mouth and let your jaw hang loosely. Move your head gently from side to side, keeping your jaw as limp as possible.

2. Stand firmly but relaxed. Raise your hands and arms up over your head, and rise on your toes. Keep stretching and try to reach higher. Let the arms slowly fall.

3. For good posture and bearing walk around the room while balancing a book on your head.

4. Yawn and say, "I'm tired; I'm going to bed."

5. Say with slow, relaxed tones, over and over:

a.
> And may there be no moaning of the bar
> When I put out to sea.

b.
> It was many and many a year ago
> In a kingdom by the sea.

c.
> An Austrian army, awfully arrayed,
> Boldly by battery besiege Belgrade.

d.
> Thou wouldst not play false,
> And yet wouldst wrongly win.

RESONANCE

Chant, hum, sing, intone. Read these passages with rich, dark, orotund quality. Get beyond the prosy sound of "Pass the pepper, please."

1.
> The curfew tolls the knell of parting day,
> The lowing herd winds slowly o'er the lea,
> The ploughman homeward plods his weary way,
> And leaves the world to darkness and to me.
>
> Now fades the glimmering landscape on the sight,
> And all the air a solemn stillness holds,
> Save where the beetle wheels his droning flight,
> And drowsy tinklings lull the distant folds.

THOMAS GRAY.

2.   God of our fathers, known of old,
            Lord of our far-flung battle-line,
        Beneath whose awful Hand we hold
            Dominion over palm and pine—
        Lord God of Hosts, be with us yet,
        Lest we forget—lest we forget!

RUDYARD KIPLING.

3. Life is a narrow vale between the cold and barren peaks of two eternities. We strive in vain to look beyond the heights. We cry aloud—and the only answer is the echo of our wailing cry. From the voiceless lips of the unreplying dead there comes no word. But in the night of Death Hope sees a star and listening Love can hear the rustle of a wing.

He who sleeps here, when dying, mistaking the approach of death for the return of health, whispered with his latest breath, "I am better now." Let us believe, in spite of doubts and dogmas, and tears and fears, that these dear words are true of all the countless dead.

ROBERT G. INGERSOLL.

4. Retreating and beating and meeting and sheeting,
        Delaying and straying and playing and spraying,
        Advancing and prancing and glancing and dancing,
        Recoiling, turmoiling and toiling and boiling,
        And gleaming and steaming and streaming and beaming,
        And rushing and flushing and brushing and gushing,
        And flapping and rapping and clapping and slapping,
        And curling and whirling and purling and twirling,
        And thumping and plumping and bumping and jumping;
        And dashing and flashing and splashing and clashing;
        And so never ending, but always descending,
        Sounds and motion forever are blending,
        All at once and all o'er, with a mighty uproar:
        And this way the water comes down at Lodore.

ROBERT SOUTHEY.

EXERCISES FOR VARIETY OF MOOD
AND QUALITY OF TONE

1.   By heaven, I had rather coin my heart,
And drop my blood for drachmas, than to wring
From the hard hands of peasants their vile trash
By any indirection.   I did send
To you for gold to pay my legions,
Which you denied me: was that done like Cassius?
Should I have answer'd Caius Cassius so?
When Marcus Brutus grows so covetous,
To lock such rascal counters from his friends,
Be ready, gods, with all your thunderbolts,
Dash him to pieces!

SHAKESPEARE.

2.   I might have saved her; now she's gone for ever!
Cordelia, Cordelia! stay a little. Ha!
What is't thou sayst? Her voice was ever soft,
Gentle and low, an excellent thing in woman.

SHAKESPEARE.

3.   And do you now put on your best attire?
And do you now cull out a holiday?
And do you now strew flowers in his way
That comes in triumph over Pompey's blood?
Be gone!
Run to your houses, fall upon your knees,
Pray to the gods to intermit the plague
That needs must light on this ingratitude.

SHAKESPEARE.

4. Engage the people by their affections, convince their reason,—and they will be loyal from the only principle that can make loyalty sincere, vigorous, or rational,—a conviction that it is their truest interest, and that their government is for their good. Constraint is the natural parent of resistance, and a pregnant proof that reason is not on the side of those who use it.

You must all remember Lucian's pleasant story; Jupiter and a countryman were walking together, conversing with great freedom and familiarity upon the subject of heaven and earth. The countryman listened with attention and acquiescence, while Jupiter strove only to convince him:—but happening to hint a doubt, Jupiter turned hastily around and threatened him with his thunder. "Ah! ah!" says the countryman, "now, Jupiter, I know that you are wrong; you are always wrong when you appeal to your thunder."

This is the case with me—I can reason with the people of England, but I cannot fight against the thunder of authority.

Thomas, Lord Erskine.

5. Once upon a time a Hare, who thought she had many friends among the other animals, heard some dogs not far away. As she was afraid they would catch her, she ran to the Horse and asked him to take her into safety. He was sorry, he said, but he was very busy; he added that she could easily get another friend to do so. She then asked the Bull to drive away the dogs with his horns. He too was sorry but he was to meet a friend at once. "No doubt the Goat will do what you want; he can do it just as well." The Goat said, however, that he feared he might hurt the Hare and suggested she ask the Ram for help. So the Hare went to the Ram. "Unfortunately," answered the Ram, "dogs eat sheep as well as hares," and he refused to risk his life. Turning to the Calf as her last chance, she begged him to help her. He replied he did not like to attempt what the older, wiser persons had refused to do. At this the Hare made one great effort to escape without aid, for the dogs were very near. As she ran off unharmed, she said to herself, "One who has many friends has really no friends."

Aesop.

6. "A merry Christmas, uncle! God save you!" cried a cheerful voice. It was the voice of Scrooge's nephew, who came upon him so quickly that this was the first intimation he had of his approach.

"Bah!" said Scrooge, "Humbug!" . . .

"Christmas a humbug, uncle!" said Scrooge's nephew. "You don't mean that, I'm sure?"

"I do," said Scrooge. "Merry Christmas! What right have you to be merry? What reason have you to be merry? You're poor enough."

"Come, then," returned the nephew gaily. "What right have you to be dismal? What reason have you to be morose? You're rich enough."

Scrooge having no better answer ready on the spur of the moment, said, "Bah!" again; and followed it up with "Humbug!"

"Don't be cross, uncle!" said the nephew.

"What else can I be," returned the uncle, "when I live in such a world of fools as this? Merry Christmas! What's Christmas-time to you but a time for paying bills without money; a time for finding yourself a year older, and not an hour richer; a time for balancing your books and having every item in 'em through a round dozen of months presented dead against you? If I could work my will," said Scrooge indignantly, "every idiot who goes about with 'Merry Christmas' on his lips should be boiled with his own pudding, and buried with a stake of holly through his heart. He should!"

CHARLES DICKENS.

7. We must recognize, then, that you may never make a nickel that you would not have made if you had never come here, that your education will not hoist you by so much as a single rung up the social ladder, and that with the finest degree in America you may have to support yourselves by pushing buttons eight hours a day. This may be disturbing to those brought up in the superstitions on which I was nourished. But they have too long obscured the true purpose of education and their true rewards. They are dangerous to educational institutions and misleading to their students. How long can colleges and universities expect donors and taxpayers to give up their money so that other people may try to learn how to make money? How long can they

expect them to part with vast sums so that the youth of America may learn to wear the right clothes, know the right people, and have a good time? And since no college or university can possibly guarantee either financial independence or social success, it perpetrates a fraud on its students if it permits them to cherish the superstitions of which I have spoken. The disappearance of these superstitions clears the way for the search for the reasons for higher education and the results that may be expected of it.

One of the most obvious answers is that higher education should help the graduate make intelligent use of the leisure which thoughtless engineers and a blind economic system have given him. Mme. de Sévigné tells the story of a little dog that belonged to Madame, the sister-in-law of Louis XIV. This little dog had one remarkable characteristic. Whenever it saw a book it would run and hide under the bed. Our population bears a distressing resemblance to this interesting animal. We spend our new and perhaps unwelcome leisure in sleep, at the movies, in playing bridge, in drinking, and in driving up and down the crowded highways, catching glimpses of the countryside between the billboards. I have tried some of these occupations and can assure you that sooner or later they begin to pall. Higher education can confer the capacity to read, to distinguish what is worth reading from what is not, to enjoy reading what is, and the habit of doing it. It can confer, too, the ability to think, to distinguish what is worth thinking about from what is not, and the habit of thinking about important things in a disciplined way.

ROBERT M. HUTCHINS.

8. Let's have a longer life and a shorter old age. . . .

Some people think that as a person grows older he requires less food. As a matter of fact, he requires more of the protective foods—fruits, vegetables, and milk in its various forms. . . .

The United States Government advises larger amounts of vitamins and minerals as one grows older. Vitamin C is one of the most important vitamins in the care of people over 45 years of age. One of the functions of this vitamin is to make more flexible the cement-like substance which holds the cells of the vessels together. If there is a deficiency of this vitamin, an artery which is undergoing the hardening process will be much more rigid and therefore more likely to break in the presence of high blood pressure or sudden exertion which puts an undue strain on the artery wall.

The average person of middle and old age, after years of habit, eats too much of the "meat, potatoes, bread and pie" routine. Persons with a tendency toward hardening of the arteries should have large quantities of such foods as green peppers, broccoli, cauliflower, cabbage, water cress, lemon, orange, and papaya, as they are rich in vitamin C.

Too frequently the man of middle age, because of certain digestive symptoms, resorts to a diet over a long period of time which is deficient in the essential protective foods. One should be certain that in dieting for whatever cause, he has an adequate supply of vitamins and minerals. . . .

I heard a remark the other day which was sufficient to make one stop and think. One man said to another, "It's too bad that Bill had to die at the age of 60." His friend answered, "Bill died at the age of 30. He was buried at the age of 60." Bill was suffering from "hidden hunger" over a period of 30 years, and finally his poor frame succumbed to malnutrition.

Let us defer old age!

THOMAS R. THORBURN.

CHAPTER XIII
The Myth of Mike Fright

Mike fright in the early days of broadcasting was as common as your Aunt Nell's habit of swooning her way through a courtship in the gay nineties. Today most cases of real mike fright are found only in the overambitious writings of those who dream up terrible tales of microphone *rigor mortis* to win space in the popular magazines.

This is not to imply that good old-fashioned nervousness isn't still with us, but we do want to debunk the general misconception that mike fright is as common as ants at a picnic. Even microphone nervousness these days is of the common garden variety and in most instances it usually passes away after a few studio appearances.

Once when we asked a great platform speaker if he ever felt nervous he playfully answered, "As nervous as a father in a maternity hospital." Then he went on to explain that he believed that most speakers have a slight case of nerves prior to getting under way.

"Stage directors are always wary of the actor who doesn't feel a bit nervous before taking the stage," explained this speaker. "Actors commonly refer to this type of nervousness as 'the spark.' Only a dead duck could face an audience without experiencing some degree of nervousness."

So if you feel even more than just a little bit nervous when first facing a microphone don't classify yourself as a hopeless victim of mike fright.

"That's all well and fine," said one young thing when we gave her this advice, "but I'm scared stiff." As a college junior she had elected radio speaking because, as she confessed, "I thought it'd be lots of fun." She had been born the timid type who wouldn't even talk back to herself if she thought it would lead to a single cross word. To make matters worse she confessed that she'd just read an article about mike fright.

"I don't know what's the matter with me," she stammered. "I'm afraid of that thing"—thing of course being her synonym for microphone. "I can't breathe and I'm trembling all over just being in the same room with it."

We could hardly believe our eyes or ears. Was this truly a case of the much publicized mike fright? Was this sweet mite of femininity to go through life hounded and haunted by the dreadful terror of once having come face to face with monster microphone?

Maybe we would yet be seeking the correct answer had not the setting been the radio studios of a coeducational institution of learning where Freddie Frats still delight in rushing to the aid of Betty Coeds in distress. Selecting the most willing of our class Beau Brummels we placed him on the opposite side of the microphone from the mike-frightened coed. It worked like a charm. She forgot that such a thing as a microphone existed and four weeks later she was not only facing the microphone with complete confidence but was actually enjoying the experience. No, the willing male didn't have to play opposite her during the four weeks; his was but a 4-minute "distraction."

In most cases of microphone nervousness, veteran radio personalities agree that it's the old, old story of self-consciousness. "Forget yourself and concentrate on what you're saying," said one station director to a speaker who complained of constant nervousness in the studio.   "If you must think, think about your audience and your style of delivery; your words and audience deserve some thought."

His was excellent advice.   Most actors will tell you that even extreme cases of nervousness can be mastered by absorbing oneself in the work at hand.   Political speakers are rarely nervous.   They are too much absorbed in proving that the other fellow deserves nothing but defeat at the polls.

To reduce studio nervousness it will be well to visit the radio station a few times prior to your first talk.   Watch other speakers.   Particularly note how they "ready" themselves for their broadcasts.   The radio veteran rarely arrives at the studio more than 15 minutes before his performance.   Can you imagine a professional stage actor walking around backstage an hour or so before the curtain rises?   To walk around a radio studio an hour before one's broadcast is just as absurd.   It's one sure way to develop a beautiful case of nerves.   Neither does the veteran radio speaker "position" himself behind the microphone until he is about ready to speak, especially if the microphone has a tendency to make him nervous.

To avoid nervousness the beginner must make every effort to relax both his mind and physical self.   Experienced radio speakers relax their minds by making it a practice to think of everything except themselves and their talk shortly before their broadcast.   It's generally the amateur who talks shop, who reads and rereads his script a few minutes prior to facing the microphone, and who works himself into a case of nerves by magnifying the importance of what he is doing.

Directors of better dramatic and comedy programs usually encourage horseplay and nonsensical chatter just before broadcast time. It may seem extremely childish and silly to the studio audience but the director knows from experience that it relaxes the actors in the interest of a better performance.

We have inferred that one reason for nervousness on the part of the stranger to Microphoneland is the fact that the studio atmosphere is comparable to that of a theater stage, not the home. Reading and rehearsing a talk at home and delivering it behind a microphone are as different as eating in the kitchen and dining in a fashionable restaurant. You probably remember the first day you started to work for a living. Everything seemed strange. New faces, new surroundings, new duties; everything was a bit confusing. To the novice microphone speaking is just like a new job. And this strangeness is certain to make you a bit nervous or, as you might say, "on edge" when first you face a microphone.

Talk with any of the more experienced announcers, actors, speakers, or singers. Ask them if they felt nervous when first they faced a microphone. The answer is always the same. Of course they felt nervous. Then ask them if they suffered a bad case of mike fright and they'll probably accuse you of reading too many magazine stories. Yes, you may find "mike fright" in the dictionary these days but that's about the only place it will pay to look for it. Forget what you've read about people who faint at the sight of a microphone. These same individuals would probably have fainted in their own homes while listening to a radio mystery thriller.

Now let's say you're ready for that first radio talk today. Of course you feel a little nervous, or maybe you don't. You've been smart and visited the radio studio a number of times during the last few weeks and you've watched other speakers, singers, and actors at work. Maybe you've talked with announcers and found them quite human. You don't arrive an hour before your scheduled broadcast nor do you wait and rush breathlessly into the studio at the last moment. Unless requested to arrive earlier you reach the station about 15 minutes before you go on the air, are assigned a studio, and immediately absorb yourself in the few details of making ready for your initial endeavor.

Before you know it, you're on the air and to your great surprise your only discomfiture was a little nervousness a few seconds before you started to talk.

It is those few seconds just before the announcer introduces you that generally accelerate any tendency to nerves. You must expect this and be prepared to meet the situation. One method of overcoming this last-minute nervousness is to interest yourself in your announcer and the way he goes about getting started. Announcers can be interesting people just before and at the start of a broadcast and their air of confidence is catching if you'll but concentrate on the way they handle things.

After you've been on the air a few times you'll find many other little ways of keeping your mind off yourself just before you start to speak, and this, according to many veterans, is the secret of getting away to a good start.

In closing this chapter let us tell you the method used by one professional radio interviewer in overcoming nervousness. He had been interviewing celebrities for more than ten years. Never once during all this time had he felt the least bit nervous, for he had devoted the last few minutes before each of his broadcasts to soothing the nerves of those whom he was about to interview. Then came the day. He inadvertently agreed to be interviewed on a women's club program. Now he was the personality.

For the first time in his radio career he found himself developing a case of nerves. As an interviewer he had been confident of his ability but in the role of a personality he seemed to lose his confidence. Station announcers and engineers gathered in the studio and control room to watch this unusual spectacle of an interviewer being interviewed. This added to the nervousness of the victim.

But he came through with unexpected impressiveness. Fortunately the clubwoman's introduction was a lengthy affair, unusually flattering; and as the verbal bouquets fell thick and fast, the interviewer executed a neat bow for each of the flowery puffs. He threw kisses to the clubwomen, the announcers, and even to the hard-boiled engineers in the control room. When the final words of the long-winded introduction had been poured into the microphone, he had everyone smiling, including himself. He was relaxed and could proceed with the interview in a friendly, chatty manner.

Mike fright, in most cases, is just plain, everyday self-consciousness intensified by an unfamiliar studio atmosphere and a lack of confidence in the work at hand. It is nothing compared to what the platform speaker or the actor may worry about. He may forget and go to pieces. You, in the studio, have a nice, sheltered spot and that sure, comforting script to support you.

CHAPTER XIV

Facing the Microphone

She was a dynamic little personality with a well-modulated, pleasing contralto voice. We expected her to perform like a veteran, but what a surprise was in store for us! No sooner had she started her talk than we knew that we were facing one of our most unpleasant studio experiences. Louder and louder, higher and higher rose her voice until she was actually shouting. We waved her back from the microphone and signaled for her to reduce the volume of her voice but to no avail. On she went, sounding more like a combination of side-show barker and hog caller than a human being.

But we hadn't heard anything. Not until after the broadcast did we get the real shock. Then it was that she explained why she had shouted into the microphone for fully 5 minutes. Her mother was visiting relatives in the northern part of Canada and she was afraid if she used her normal, soft, well-modulated voice her mother wouldn't hear her. Yes, they say anything can happen in a radio studio and it generally does, particularly in the studios of the smaller stations.

How about your local political speakers? Are they chock-full of the old-time oratorical bombast or do they more wisely remember that the radio audience is a family audience accustomed to voices pitched at the conversational level? And how about your local station announcer? Does he try to force those silly commercials down your throat with the commanding voice of a theater usher or does he employ the smoother, friendly, fireside style of President Roosevelt?

When you face that microphone remember that you're not addressing a mass meeting, you're talking to a family group. Work for a pleasant, friendly voice and, if you're reading from script, talk as if you were speaking from notes, not as if you were reading the last will and testament of your late Aunt Sarah or delivering an old-fashioned Memorial Day address.

Oh, if only the local politicians, the announcers who shout their wares, the would-be orators, and the many others who seem to confuse a microphone with a megaphone could only hear themselves as others hear them. They sound about as sincere as a Jap ambassador in Washington.

A few years ago we attended a convention in a near-by city. Most of the speakers were much above the ordinary. One in particular stood out like Lincoln at Gettysburg. Weeks later we read in the radio offerings that this same speaker was to appear on one of the popular forum programs. We rushed home to hear him. What a disappointment! This couldn't possibly be the same fellow we had heard at the convention. It must be another man with a similar name. Reading from a prepared script this convention Lincoln sounded like a schoolboy reciting *Hamlet* for the first time. What had happened? We must have the answer. So we wrote to the director of the forum.

"I'm a speaker, not a script reader," he had told the forum director when informed that wartime restrictions would necessitate his speaking from prepared material. "I never speak from a prepared address, I just talk."

He knew that to read prepared material so that your listeners will feel that you are talking extemporaneously is the golden secret of good radio speaking. Not being able to see you, the radio audience doesn't know you are reading from script unless you sound as if you are reading. Unfortunately, 90 per cent of inexperienced radio speakers seem to be wholly unaware of this most important fact. It is the worst weakness of all tyros.

As one veteran announcer put it, "The radio listener likes to feel that you are talking to him, not to a million others. To listen to most radio speakers you'd think talking was a lost art." When we asked this announcer for his advice to radio speakers anxious to overcome this most common fault, he said, "Tell them to be natural, to be themselves."

Of course, he didn't mean exactly what he said. If a person is naturally ungrammatical and sloppy in his everyday conversation it would hardly be advisable for him to be his natural self. But this announcer had the right idea.

Americans like to hear a man talk when he has something to say and knows how to say it. They have very little use for polished oratory. In listening to a speaker they like to feel that he is a regular fellow, not a stuffed shirt; the type of person they'd gladly invite to their home for an evening's talkfest.

"I won't have any trouble with the words right in front of me but I could never ad-lib," said a speaker who had been asked to lengthen his radio talk an extra minute. He was one of the poorest microphone speakers we've ever heard. Yes, the words were right in front of him and he read them as if he were reading a book to his grandmother.

Many amateur actors have the mistaken idea that radio acting is much easier than stage acting. Why? Because the words are all in front of one. Reading words and acting are two different things and the speaker to be a success on the air today must be a "voice actor." Watch an experienced radio dramatic group in action. Yes, the words are all written out on paper but those smiles and mannerisms they put into their lines aren't on the type-written pages. They aren't reading words. They're acting. They're putting life and feeling into every line; their whole personality vibrates in harmony with the part they are portraying. That's what we mean by "voice acting."

A few months ago we had the pleasure of working with a real voice actor. He is one of the most forceful radio preachers we've ever heard. Although he has no studio audience, his facial expressions and gestures are similar to those of the platform speaker. He knows that if the radio listener is to feel the smile in the voice his face must register that smile. He has learned the art of making his audience of the "blind" see and feel not only his words but the gestures behind them.

Suggesting to one of our theological friends that many a radio preacher could learn a great deal by watching this man in action, this theologian remarked, "Oh, he just does that for effect. He's showing off; just an actor." That remark summed up just how little that particular theologian knew about radio speaking. Little did he know that all good radio speakers must be good voice actors. Our radio preacher gives his words life and feeling and he makes his audience feel them. He believes that God's words merit life and feeling.

Stirring the feelings of an audience a few feet away is one thing, and it's not easy; but putting that same feeling into a piece of metal so that it will emotionally stimulate listeners miles away is a task that defeats many ambitious radio speakers. Maybe you think that we are putting too much stress on this point. Well, let's put it another way. If we could give you but one piece of advice before you face a microphone, we'd say, "Talk and make them feel what you say; don't read or make a speech."

Radio has demonstrated that reading aloud is almost a lost art. Unless you have been reading fairy tales to the children you probably haven't read aloud for any length of time in years. You probably never practiced reading aloud in an effort to make your reading sound as if you were ad-libbing the material. That, however, is what you must do if your prepared material is to sound like a talk. Sounds easy, but try it.

Take, for example, the most exciting experience in your life. Tell it in about 200 words. Then write 200 words in the same style that you normally used in telling it. Now read the prepared material. Place a friend in a near-by room to listen to both the ad-libbing and the script reading. Don't permit the friend to remain in the same room with you for that permits him to see your facial expressions. Remember, the radio audience "sees" you only with its ears. If your friend doesn't see any difference between the ad-libbed story and the script reading, you are a natural radio reader. Don't be discouraged, however, if you are informed that your script reading lacked the life and feeling of your ad-lib version. A test in a college class of seventy-five students produced just one natural reader.

If you really want to improve your radio reading ability, secure copies of professional radio talks as given on such programs as America's Town Meeting of the Air. Read them aloud as often as you have the opportunity. Work to make them sound as if you were ad-libbing the material.

See how near you come to equaling the work of the professionals who appear on this popular weekly program.

With this advice in mind, let's step into your local radio station. We'd like to hear you read a few paragraphs and also listen to the tonal quality of your speaking voice. Voices differ considerably in volume and clearness, and the control-room engineer is sure to want a voice level. This is to determine your correct position at the microphone. If you are like most beginners, you don't know the difference between the front and the back of a microphone. It's not necessary that the radio speaker know the secrets and the mechanical workings of these mysterious gadgets, but it is well to know that most microphones are unidirectional, bidirectional, or nondirectional. The speaker's microphone is usually of the unidirectional type—"live" on one side only. To make you more comfortable we'll use the table type of unidirectional microphone so that you may read from a sitting position.

"How far should I be from this microphone?" Ah, we expected that question. Eight to ten inches is the answer. You'll probably notice that we've placed the microphone directly in front of you. Most voices sound best when, in the jargon of the radio studio, they are directly "on the beam." This merely means that your voice is directly hitting the most sensitive part of the microphone. Just make yourself comfortable and relax. If we weren't with you, the "positioning" of the microphone would be taken care of by the announcer or engineer.

May we suggest that you remove that paper clip from your script? It will help eliminate paper rattle, and you don't want to remind the audience that you're reading from prepared material—remember? Paper rattle and unnecessary throat clearing are two things that the listeners will never miss, so if you feel like clearing your throat, do it right now before you go into action.

Now the engineer is ready for that voice level. Just keep reading until you are signaled to stop. We're leaving you now to join the engineer in the control room. We're not interested in how you sound in the studio. We want to hear your voice over the control-room loud-speaker, for that approximates what the listeners will hear when you are on the air.

Your exact microphone position will be determined after we hear your voice in the control room. Okay, my friend, the microphone is yours. Take it away.

If you are like most beginners we'll be greeted with the same old question the minute you've finished reading. "How did I sound?" And, if you made the mistakes common to novices, here is the list:

You read too fast.

You forgot and nervously cleared your throat just before you started.

You failed to put any bodily action into your words. You didn't even smile when you told that joke.

You occasionally looked off the script as you might if speaking on the platform. Keep your eyes on your material.

You talked to the side of the microphone at times. Stay "on the beam."

Your voice lacked flexibility.

Your interpretation was weak.

You hit the microphone too hard with those first few words.

At times your voice was "in the mud" (radio term meaning "too little volume").

You nervously smacked your lips.

You failed to breathe properly and we could hear you "taking in" air.

Your pronunciation of certain words was incorrect.

You didn't sound sure of yourself and your words.

You obviously were reading, not talking as you naturally talk.

Hopeless? Certainly not. You just had the self-consciousness of most beginners and it showed in your work. No, you won't attempt to correct at once all the faults in your first talk. That would only make for confusion. Eliminate your weaknesses one at a time.

If possible, have a recording made of your first talk. This will enable you to hear your own mistakes. In another chapter we'll have more to say about voice recordings and how they may be used to improve your microphone work.

In the meantime listen to speakers, particularly those broadcasting from the smaller stations. Learn to recognize radio speech weaknesses in others. It will help you to correct your own.

CHAPTER XV

You're on the Air

You've just been on the air for the first time, let us say. When you asked them at the station how it sounded, they merely said, "Okay." They didn't praise; they didn't criticize. They just said, "Okay."

You go home to the natural-born critic you married. Does she join the okay chorus? She does not.

"You were terrible. You didn't sound a bit like yourself and"—but before she can tell you the worst the telephone rings and you rush to answer it.

It's good old George. He takes 10 minutes to tell you that he heard every word and that your talk was great.

Before bedtime, Aunt Kate, Uncle Joe, your mother and father, the neighbors next door, and a dozen other friends have telephoned, and they all say you were swell.

But let's hear what your wife said after you got through talking with George. You particularly remember that part which went something like this, "But you want me to tell the truth, don't you? What did they say at the station?" You tell her that they said it was okay.

"But they didn't say it was good, did they?" You admit that they didn't and you're just getting ready to tell her that they didn't say it was terrible either when she interrupts you with something like this:

"It's too bad that you didn't have them make a record of your talk; you'd get the surprise of your life."

189

It's at this point that you lead with your ace. "But they made a record," you chirp, "and they're going to play it for me tomorrow."

As usual she trumps your ace with, "Well, just wait until you hear the record."

The next afternoon you visit the station and you hear your own voice for the first time. To put it mildly, you're a little disappointed in what you hear.

Months later you know the real truth. You've been on the air a number of times. Even your wife thinks you're doing much better, and you feel pretty good. You've learned much about evaluating personal reactions to your talks, and you now know that no respectable studio personnel ever say anything except okay about a speaker's performance unless that speaker is so good that they can truthfully praise him.

Thanks to one of the boys at the station, you're really on the right track now. He helped a lot when he said he thought you were speaking a little too fast. You were quite surprised when he checked your rate of speed with a stop watch and you learned that you were speaking more than 170 words a minute.

"That's the speed our news announcers usually employ," he said. "It's much too fast for a speaker to talk. President Roosevelt and other accomplished radio speakers average about 130 to 140 words a minute, and they're masters of the rhetorical pause."

"Rhetorical pause! Beautiful expression," you say to yourself, "but what does it mean in my language?" Today you call it "the pause that refreshes." You've learned to pause after certain words and groups of words in the interest of additional emphasis and better breathing. You've also learned that speaking at an average rate of speed of about 140 words a minute makes for better enunciation, flexibility of voice interpretation, and improved quality of voice.

"A nervous, fast-talking speaker is usually what I call a 'Johnny One-note'," said a studio veteran. "A Johnny One-note is a fellow who fails to use the speaking range of his voice. Of course, Walter Winchell uses speed to style his delivery, but even this radio race horse uses other tricks of the trade to keep his Hooper rating in the upper brackets."

Begin slowly. This tends to relieve any nervous tension and gives your voice a more friendly, conversational tone.

By this time you've probably learned that all emphasis is no emphasis, and you don't try to emphasize every other word. You underscore certain words in your script before starting to talk. Stress, attack, and projection are necessary but so is variety of rhythm. Steady pounding is monotonous and fails to indicate differences between major and minor ideas.

Not only should you underscore important words and sentences but you should put a mark before all long sentences. All good announcers mark their copy to warn themselves when long sentences or long paragraphs may put an additional tax on their breathing apparatus. They pause frequently—not merely at commas—but wherever the thought units indicate a natural pause.

Here is a sentence taken at random from a speech by Winston Churchill. It might be marked as follows for the natural pauses that will allow frequent breathing without violating the sense of the passage:

Had not this ruler/and his government/severed themselves from the Allies/who rescued their country from extinction/in the late war,//and had they not sought refuge/in what has been proved to be fatal neutrality,//then the French and the British armies/at the outset/might well have saved/not only Belgium/but perhaps even Holland.

Longer pauses are indicated by double lines. Of course, more units may be given on one breath—fewer pauses may be made—at the discretion of the speaker, but the principle is clear. Study every passage carefully to avoid breathless and strained speaking.

If you stumble over a word or mispronounce it, don't be disturbed. Keep right on going as if nothing had happened. "If you attempt to correct yourself after mispronouncing a word," says the announcer, "you tell everyone you've made a mistake, but if you keep right on reading, it's always possible that the listener will think he heard incorrectly."

You've learned something else if you've studied experienced radio speakers in the studio. To get life and spontaneity into their talks they let go with the same gestures and action that would supplement their words in lively, informal conversation. So now you smile, we hope, nod your head, move your hands and arms, and do anything else that will help to put more feeling into what you are saying. It may seem funny to those looking at you from outside the studio, but what do you care? You're talking to millions, maybe, and you want them to feel your words as if you were present and talking to each one eye to eye.

You may have seen a speaker remove his necktie and unbutton his shirt collar before he started broadcasting. Perhaps that better tone quality he is getting is traceable to the new freedom enjoyed by the throat muscles. At least it makes him look very professional at the microphone.

Was your first talk too long? Did you fear that you could never finish that final page? If so, you have no doubt learned to use provisional cuts. It's too bad all amateur speakers don't know enough to practice this simple device of marking off a couple of less important paragraphs near the end of the script. Cutting them out when the time is short saves you a lot of trouble and worry.

Practice using a stop watch to time your material. You will find this method much better than using the living-room clock. Be sure to check your stop watch every now and then or it may fool you some time. If you forget to stop your watch when you are cutting a paragraph from your talk you may discover, by the time you awaken to your oversight, that your timing is worse than it would have been had you been using an old-fashioned sundial.

When you don't need to cut, you may still need a "cushion," that is, an additional paragraph or two which you should always have in reserve in case your material doesn't fill the required time.

The cushion is usually added to the last page of your talk as extra paragraphs. Good speakers are usually prepared with both the provisional cut and the cushion. That is why they can end their talks within 5 or 10 seconds of the allotted time.

Most professional radio speakers also time-check each page. By placing the total time at the bottom of each sheet, all they have to do as they finish reading each sheet is to glance at the studio clock. Should they speak a little faster or a little slower during the broadcast than they did when they time-checked their material, they can adjust their reading time while on the air. Some professionals total the reading time after every paragraph on the final page of their material; especially those who pride themselves on ending "right on the nose,"—on the split second of the allotted time.

It may appear a little too professional to have a glass of cold water handy when speaking on the air but the time may come when you'll need a little sip to give that frog in your throat a chance to jump one way or the other.

We recall a congressman who would have given half his district one evening for a jigger of aqua pura. What got into his throat we'll never know, but to say that he nearly strangled at the microphone would be putting it mildly. Had we been blessed with television we should probably have seen the announcer rushing madly out of the studio for a glass of water, but minus the visual we had to be content to listen to the pride of his constituents gasp for breath and struggle against time in the hope that he'd still be among those present by the time relief arrived.

Suddenly there was silence. Was the congressman being revived with the water or had it arrived too late? Seconds seemed like minutes, and then back on the air came his voice, seemingly none the worse for the terrifying experience.

Whenever a speaker has throat trouble while facing a microphone he should remember that no law of the land prevents him from requesting a glass of water. Maybe the congressman was afraid that he might be breaching parliamentary law to stop in the midst of his speech and make such a common-sense request, but it is better to be ruled out of order than strangled out of existence.

Most speakers make too much fuss about mishaps. They fear any letdown in their too formal manner at the microphone. Mayor X was like that. He was campaigning for reelection and was hitting on all eight when Mistress Mistake tipped the hand that was holding his script and scattered the pages in all directions.

Frantically he scrambled to pick up the pages. His face flushed crimson. Breathing harder and harder he finally managed to recover all the pages, started to read again, and then burst into cuss words that Sherman could have used while marching through Georgia. Page four had been misplaced before page three. Shuffling the pages brought no better results but it did bring another fiery outbreak that nearly knocked the ears off the control-room engineer.

Whether the mayor won his reelection we don't know, but we do know that, had he calmly and good-naturedly explained his predicament, he would have had the good will of all his listeners. Everybody admires the man of poise who is not mortified or defeated because he happened to break a piece of formal etiquette. Why be a slave to custom when everybody's shouting for the bigger freedoms?

CHAPTER XVI

The Voice Is the Thing?

"Everyone tells me that I have a wonderful telephone voice and that I ought to be on the air," enthusiastically babbled a youngster sitting across from us when we asked him why he was so eager to get into radio. In the minds of those whose knowledge of radio is generally limited to listening to a few of their favorite programs, the voice is not only the thing; it is everything.

Let's agree right now that a good voice is a mighty valuable asset to an announcer, speaker, or singer, but just because one has what his friends may term "a wonderful telephone voice" is no guarantee that the voice when used behind a microphone will be equally as charming. The ordinary telephone line in comparison with the lines used in broadcasting just doesn't compare. Many of the higher frequencies in the speaking voice never reach the ear of a telephone listener owing to the limitation in frequencies carried by the average telephone equipment. The telephone lines used in broadcasting have much higher frequencies. The pitch of that charming low telephone voice may sound much higher when coming from a loud-speaker. This is a simple, nontechnical explanation of why many telephone voices sound less pleasing on the air. There are other reasons too.

Using a telephone mouthpiece may appear, to a novice, much the same as talking into a microphone, but experienced radio speakers will tell you that a microphone does "tricks" with the voice that the telephone has never heard about.   These same speakers could also tell you that a good radio speaker can do "tricks" with a microphone that would be totally lost on a telephone mouthpiece.   Yet, month after month, year after year, we are greeted by ambitious youngsters with "wonderful" telephone voices and we have to tell them these painful truths.

There is another group, generally ambitious parents, who seem to believe that all one has to do is to listen to their darling speak a few lines and, presto, the verdict as to the radio possibilities of the voice is immediately forthcoming.   Just a few days ago a mother accompanied by her daughter came in to see us.   "I think my daughter has a splendid voice and I thought you might help her get started in radio.   I've brought along something for her to read."   She then gave the girl a poem to recite and before we could act in self-defense the daughter was chilling us with Whittier's "Snowbound."   We'd survived many similar ordeals, so our training enabled us to stand this one.   Then we informed the mother that a voice in a room sounds very different from the same voice at a microphone.   According to the latest reliable reports both mother and daughter were heading in the direction of a radio station.

Let's assume that our reports were correct and that the program manager took the afternoon off just to listen to the recitation of "Snowbound."   After hearing her voice at a microphone, could he correctly evaluate the future radio possibilities of the girl's voice as an asset to a possible successful career in broadcasting?   The answer is "no."

How, you may ask, does one go about finding out whether he or she has a good radio voice, a voice with that certain something which is sure to lead to success in radio? Certainly, you say, the program manager could tell a girl whether she had a good or a poor radio voice. You're right in one respect, but wrong in another. If by a good radio voice you mean a voice that sounds good over a loud-speaker, then you are right in feeling that the program manager could easily render a decision. On the other hand, if by a good radio voice you mean a voice that will win the approval of the listening audience, you are asking for a verdict which only that radio audience can give.

Let's put it another way. When is a voice a good radio voice? We can hear many professional radiomen answer, "When that voice pleases the majority of those in the radio audience." Other program managers will insist that the quality of the voice is relatively unimportant provided the speaker has something to say and says it with that certain something in the voice which wins listeners. This school believes that speech instructors place too much importance on tonal quality, articulation, and interpretation.

One of these program managers cites the experience of a woman who started on his station years ago and who has one of the largest feminine audiences in his section of the country:

The first few broadcasts by this woman brought hundreds of letters virtually demanding that we take "that terrible voice off the air." Even today we receive occasional letters criticizing it, and many listeners have told me personally that her voice is the worst they've ever listened to.

What's the answer? Frankly, I don't know but I do know that this woman has a capacity listening audience. Of course, what she says and the way she says it have something to do with her success but she'll never be given the prize for the best radio voice in this neck of the woods. I'm just glad that we didn't attempt to evaluate the possibilities in her voice and judge it as "not any good for radio" when first she auditioned at our station.

How about the beauty of tone quality in the voices of such successful radio personalities as Bob Hope, Fred Allen, Jack Benny, Fibber McGee, Walter Winchell, and others too numerous to mention.   They'd hardly steal first prize away from speakers like President Roosevelt, Milton J. Cross, or even George Denny, if tonal quality and diction were the only factors to be considered for good radio voice work.

Maybe we could say that a good radio voice must have personality and let it go at that.   But let's be more specific. Let's assume that you have a smooth, soft, pleasing tonal quality but your voice sounds lifeless on the air.   We might say that your voice lacks force or projection.   You've probably heard many voices on the air whose tonal quality was pleasing but they didn't command or hold your attention and you soon dialed to another station.

We don't just sit right in front of a loud-speaker and give our undivided attention to a speaker.   Much of our listening is of the subconscious type.   A speaker must hold our attention through life in his voice.   Don't Bob Hope, Jack Benny, and Walter Winchell have life in their voices? They stimulate the listener's emotions by the feeling and force they put into their lines.   We can just hear you saying, "But I'm a speaker, not a comedian or actor."

Sorry.   All good radio speakers are actors.   And, though you are not expected to equal the wit of a Hope or a Benny, learn how to work a little humor into your talk; never forget that most people love to laugh.

Now how does the amateur go about getting life into his voice work?   Force and feeling in voice do not mean that one has to resort to loudness or shouting.   Mark this point carefully. Many political speakers attempt to gain force through shouting and they fail miserably. A whisper well placed in a talk will make the audience feel the force of a remark much more sometimes than the loudest shout. The thing to remember is that they must "feel" what you are saying, and this feeling is gained by the amount of feeling (not loudness) that you put into your voice work.

Another important factor in radio speaking might come under the title of "mood." One of the most successful announcers on the air summed up this matter of mood one day when he said, "I may have a headache, all my creditors may be sitting on my doorstep, my wife may have just left me, and my house may be burning down but when I go on the air my mood must be the mood of the announcement I'm making."

A speaker must study his material carefully before facing a microphone and determine the changes of mood, for moods may vary in different paragraphs. He may be exciting his audience to laughter in one paragraph, and in the next he may be working for their tears. The three major emotions may be summed up in one successful actor's answer to a newspaper interviewer's question, "What one piece of advice would you give to the beginner seeking fame and fortune on the stage?" "Make 'em laugh, cry, or thrill to your lines," said this actor. "People come to the theater wrapped in different moods. It's an actor's job to put them in the mood of the play by first putting himself in the mood of his lines."

Emotion, not reason, governs most of our actions, according to psychologists. A good radio speaker knows this, and the mood of his delivery is aimed to stimulate his audience emotionally just as the mood in music stimulates an audience when correctly interpreted by a great musician.

Check each paragraph of your talk before you face a microphone. Determine the mood of each sentence and each paragraph. Then interpret that mood so deeply that it is felt by every listener. Note that we say, "deeply." Wasn't it Montesquieu who, in flaying some speakers, said, "What too many orators want in depth they give you in length"? Yes, there must be depth of feeling and depth in the material content of your talk. Watch the mood in your lines and in your voice.

If your voice lacks the so-called beautiful tonal quality there is something else that may help make your talks so interesting that the audience will forget the weakness in tonal beauty. Professional radio speakers refer to this particular help as "styling." Walter Winchell has styling aplenty. So have Fred Allen, Raymond Gram Swing, Boake Carter, and many other well-known radio personalities. Fred Allen capitalizes on the nasal quality of his voice. In other words, make your major weakness your major strength by styling. Style may also be obtained in speed of delivery. Winchell's speed and life in delivery force the average listener to become wholly unconscious of the weakness in the direction of tonal quality and articulation.

Style and your radio personality are closely associated. You'd know the voice of Raymond Gram Swing if his name was never announced. As far as the perfect speaking voice goes, he leaves much to be desired, but when it comes to styling he is a past master of the art. One favorite sports announcer styles his delivery by clipping his words. He snaps them at you in such a way that even the description of a sunset behind a football stadium would be a thing of action as well as beauty.

Listen to these stylists on the air. Don't imitate but analyze your own speaking voice and determine which style best suits your own personality and delivery. Remember styling is a trade-mark to the radio speaker and it is worth much if properly developed.

By this time you must have come to the conclusion that styling and timing have much in common. Exactly what is timing? Maybe Bob Hope's rise to fame may best illustrate the value of good timing. It may also serve to give you a nondictionary definition of the word as used in radio. It's no secret in radio circles that Bob Hope was not an overnight sensation when he came from the legitimate stage to radio. One of his first radio contracts found him much of a novice in this thing called radio timing. On the stage, Bob could wisecrack a line and then wait for the audience to laugh or sit on its hands. He knew his stage timing from *A* to *Z*. On the air things were different. He didn't know when his listeners were laughing at his gags nor when they were hissing them. He timed his gags too fast or too slow. When too fast the audience would miss many of his funniest quips. When too slow, his wisecracks seemed labored. Bob well knew that old expression, "Art is where all traces of labor have been eliminated." He must have a different type of material from that used on the stage. It must be so written that it would be timed for the radio audience.

Bob studied the timing of other comedians. He secured veteran radio writers who knew their radio timing. His radio success started from this point. Today his style and timing are the envy of his competitors, and that the audience reacts favorably to both is evidenced by his constant top position in all radio polls.

A platform speaker may walk the entire length of the platform without uttering a word. You don't miss his words for his action has taken the place of his words.

On the air, if you walked away from the microphone for a canter around the studio, the radio audience might decide that you'd gone home and dial you out for the evening. Your actions wouldn't take the place of your words. In radio timing you must make your audience "see" your actions through their ears. Care must also be taken that the timing of lines is such that they are easily assimilated by the ear. Stage lines, accompanied by gestures, may be shot very fast and yet be comprehended by the audience. On the air you are robbed of this visual help; at least until television arrives.

Voice is the thing according to many radio veterans, but you must not forget that a good voice is but one of the qualifications needed for success on the air. If you haven't a golden voice, don't think that you have no possibilities in Microphoneland. Remember what we have said about many of radio's headliners. They employed mood, timing, styling, and other radio tricks to offset their weakness in tonal quality. You can do the same thing if you're willing to work and work hard.

Radio-station managers say that the male voice tone is at its best when the speaker's range is baritone or baritone-base. Tenors rarely make good announcers. The contralto has the call among women, and we've never heard of a soprano announcer, although it is quite possible that this exception to the rule occasionally makes a hit with the radio audience as distributor of beauty hints, cooking recipes, or feminine fancies.

The soprano or tenor speaking voice with a high level of pitch may improve the tonal quality of the voice by employing a slower delivery. Speak fast and you'll note the tendency of the voice to rise. Even a Gracie Allen loses some of the dumbness in her characterization when she slows down. Dennis Day, Jack Benny's singer, also loses much of his gullibility in talk when he fails to shoot his lines at a speed of from 170 to 180 words per minute. Speed in voice at the microphone tends to emphasize the higher frequencies and robs the voice of the lower tones preferred by the average listener.

Should the pitch level be too low the speaker will do well to speak a little faster or increase the force and clarity of his enunciation. "In the mud" is the radio expression for the deep, bassy, unpleasant throaty voice, and the slower one speaks the more "mud" creeps into the radio voice. Most "mudders" fail to use the full tonal range of the voice. If they played the piano, they'd probably play only on the lower notes. Use all the notes in your voice, no matter what your speaking range may be, but for the deep bass voice this advice should be doubled and redoubled.

CHAPTER XVII
Use Recordings and Be Your Own Critic

Some years ago we asked a well-known radio speaker what he liked best about radio. "The fact that I never have to listen to myself," he laughingly snapped back. Today that same speaker listens to himself daily and enjoys it. He has a recording made of each broadcast and is forever trying to improve some little weakness in his delivery. "I don't know how we ever got along without recordings in the early days of radio. To think that I was on the air for four years and never knew how terrible I sounded," he told us the other day.

This radio veteran majored in speech and English while at college but had never heard his own voice until his broadcasts were recorded. "I had one of the best speech instructors in the country but I learned more about my own voice in listening to one 15-minute recording than I learned in college for four years. To work on the air these days without hearing recordings of your work is like talking to yourself in your sleep. Your wife may know what you're saying but you don't. All radio speakers should use recordings of their broadcasts to improve their work." Such was the advice of this radio veteran and we heartily endorse it. If it is true that one picture is worth a thousand words, it is just as true that to hear one's own voice work is worth many critical suggestions on the part of others.

"But that doesn't sound like my voice," said a fair young thing when she heard her first recording. Like almost all of us she was surprised at what she heard. We had to explain that she never actually hears her own voice as others hear it. "But I hear myself every time I speak, don't I?" Not until her mother had heard the recording and assured the daughter that the recorded voice sounded exactly like the girl's speaking voice was she convinced that what we had said was the truth.

This is just one of the many reasons why the beginner will do well to have a voice recording made as soon as possible. To know how your voice sounds to others is the first step in the direction of good voice work on the air.

Of course it is preferable that the recording be a faithful reproduction of your voice. There are both good and bad recordings. That is why it is wise to have members of your family listen to any you have made. If they assure you that the recorded voice is an exact duplicate of your speaking voice you may feel assured that you have a quality recording. If possible, have your first recording made by experienced recording engineers in a regular recording studio. Most broadcasting stations have good equipment for this work but few stations will make recordings for beginners.

That's all very well, you say, for those who live near recording studios but how about those who live in small towns and cities where such studios are scarcer than Eskimos in New York?

Don't be discouraged. Thousands of portable recording machines are owned by schools, colleges, radio repair shops, distributors of sound systems, individuals who make their own motion pictures, and even men and women who make a hobby of amateur recording. The records may not be of the highest quality but you can learn many things from studying records made on portable machines. In rare cases some of these recordings may even equal the quality of professional platters.

First, remember that you are making recordings not only to hear how your voice sounds to others but to check your speaking speed, style of delivery, timing, pacing, and all the other qualities necessary for good radio voice work. If the tonal quality of the recording is poor, it still ensures a valuable check on these other things. Fair recordings are better than none.

Let's say that you are one of the more fortunate and live in a city that supports at least one good recording studio. When you inquire as to the cost of such work you'll find that good recordings of your voice will cost about $5 up. Don't expect this price to include $100 worth of professional speech advice, a course on how to face a microphone, and a money-back guarantee that the recording will land you a thousand-a-week contract with your local radio station.

Professional recording studios supply the disks, studios, equipment, and engineers. They expect you to know what you want, and when you do they'll cooperate wholeheartedly in seeing that you get it.

"Oh, I just want a record of my voice," says a young man with secret ambitions to become a Bill Stern, a Milton J. Cross, or a Raymond Gram Swing. Knowing absolutely nothing about recordings he thinks he's hearing a foreign language if he's asked such questions as, "Do you want a 6-inch, 8-inch, 10-inch, 12-inch, or 16-inch disk? Do you want it recorded 33⅓ r.p.m. or 78 r.p.m.? Shall we record inside out or outside in? Will you want any pressings?"

Recording disks come in various sizes. The size required will depend upon the number of minutes to be recorded.

If the recording is for a phonograph playback, it should be recorded at 78 r.p.m. (engineering term for "revolutions per minute"). For broadcasting purposes it will be less expensive to record material at 33⅓ r.p.m. Broadcast platters are usually recorded from the inside out; phonograph playbacks, from the outside in. If duplicates or pressings are to be made, the studio will advise that they be processed before the record is played back for hearing. This ensures better quality duplicates.

Approximate Recording Time of Disk Sizes

Disk size, inches	33⅓ r.p.m.	78 r.p.m.
6		1 min.
8		2 min.
10	3½ min.	3½ min.
12	7½ min.	5½ min.
16	17 min.	

Note: Recorded 96 lines per inch.

Not all recording studios will ask these questions, but to know the answers will probably save you money, time, and energy. When you come out of the studio with the record under your arm you'll be better satisfied with what you've purchased. Don't visit a recording studio and say, "I'd like to have a record of my voice; you know what I want."

A few months ago a friend came to us with a recording. He was to talk for 5 minutes on the subject of "Child Delinquency." "I've recited a little poetry and a few scenes from *Hamlet*. It's not very good but it'll give you a pretty good idea of my speaking voice, don't you think?"

When we asked why he hadn't recorded a few paragraphs of his talk he told us that poetry and dramatic readings always demonstrated his voice to best advantage. "Excellent," we quipped, "if your radio program included poetry or readings from *Hamlet*, but you're talking on 'Child Delinquency.' Or are we wrong?"

No, we weren't wrong. Seeing the point immediately, he tossed the recording into a near-by wastebasket and said, "Where do we go from here?"

Within a few minutes we had him facing a microphone. He'd forgotten all about poetry and *Hamlet*. He was ad-libbing a talk on "Child Delinquency." Note that he was not reading from script; he was ad-libbing. Did he have his script with him? He did. Fine. Now he was told to ad-lib 2 minutes on the subject of child delinquency and then read the first five paragraphs of his prepared material. We wanted him to hear the difference between his ad-libbing and his reading from script. Yes, unknown to him, we were making a recording.

What a surprise he received when we played the record. His ad-libbing was excellent. His natural, conversational style was friendly and pleasing. Tonal quality of voice and interpretation were much above average, but the minute the recording reached the portion that he'd read from script he sounded formal and artificial. "I don't sound like myself at all when I read from script. Even the tone of my voice sounds different." He was truly discouraged.

We assured him that 95 per cent of radio beginners have the same trouble and that quite a few professional platform speakers find script reading at a microphone rather difficult.

"But is there anything I can do to make my script reading sound as smooth and natural as my ad-libbing?" His face had a most hopeless expression.

"Listen to President Roosevelt. Tune in all radio speakers. Make a study of those who sound as though they were reading from script and those who talk as though they were ad-libbing. President Roosevelt almost always reads as though he were making up every word as he goes along but he rarely faces a microphone without prepared material," we said.

We then went on to explain that the best way to make script reading sound like ad-libbing was to read prepared material as if every word was coming from the brain and not from a piece of paper. When one ad-libs it is necessary to pause and think what is to be said next. With the words all on paper the speaker is being pulled along at a constant pace. It isn't necessary to make "thought pauses."

Professionals refer to President Roosevelt as "the master of the rhetorical pause." He sounds as though he were stopping to think before expressing a certain thought. He also uses the pause between words in a sentence. This has the effect not only of throwing tremendous emphasis on these words but of giving him a natural conversational style.

To get a better idea of pausing in the interest of naturalness we advised our friend to study the average person's daily conversation. Most people find it difficult to express themselves in a clear, concise manner. The tongue is capable of running much faster than the brain can furnish words. What happens? In natural conversation we pause many times right in the middle of a sentence. We are virtually stopped for lack of words to express our thoughts.

Natural conversation is seldom easily fluent and rhythmic. To speak well we must pause frequently to select forceful words. Brilliant words on paper may be read by almost anyone without constant pauses. This is the chief reason why prepared material has a tendency to destroy the naturalness of the speaker. It robs him of his personality of speech by making a "parrot reader" out of him. We told our friend to write these words on paper. "Fourscore and seven years ago our fathers brought forth on this continent a new nation, conceived in liberty, and dedicated to the proposition that all men are created equal." On another piece of paper we wrote, "About eighty-seven years ago we created a new nation and called it the United States of America. We had fought for our liberty and we were determined to see to it that all men were given equal rights."

"Read the first lines of Lincoln's masterful address and then read this crude rewrite," we said, handing him what we had written.

He read both aloud. We recorded his readings. When the recording was played back it was evident that his reading of the first few lines of Lincoln's address sounded much more like a speech than did our more conversational rewrite. Now he had another reason why so many radio talks sound like speeches. Written for oratorical delivery, the sentence phrasing makes many radio talks sound as though the speaker was just parading his ability to use all the "pretty" soul-stirring words in the dictionary.

"Write your talks in a conversational style and then read them as though you were making up each sentence as you read." We were trying to sum up our advice in the simplest way possible.

Yes, our friend had many other weaknesses, particularly in the direction of lack of force, timing, inflection, and voice acting, but it is very unwise to correct more than one fault at a time.

Don't attempt to record your complete talk. Record about three or four pages. Select your most glaring weakness and then work to correct it. Then make another recording. Check to see that your greatest weakness has been eliminated. Not until this has been done should you attempt to correct your next most serious fault. In most cases this one-at-a-time method will work wonders. To attempt to correct a number of weaknesses at the same time is confusing and difficult and usually tends to discourage a beginner. We can't stress this fact too forcefully.

If not sure of your worst faults, why not play your first recording to a few willing listeners? Of course, if you know of a good speech instructor or veteran radio speaker willing to criticize your work, it will pay you well to secure professional advice regarding your greatest weaknesses.

Just one word of caution. If you ask the advice of nonprofessionals, don't put them in a critical state of mind prior to playing the recording. Play the record and then ask for a list of your worst faults.

There is one other way in which recordings can be used to excellent advantage; that is, to determine style of delivery and pitch in voice. We've already told you how important pace and speed are to good tonal quality. Style of delivery and pitch in voice are just as important. Here is a piece of copy we give to many beginners. By recording a reading of it, the novice can hear just how his voice sounds at different rates of speed. The first paragraph should be delivered at the normal conversational rate of speed usually used by the beginner. The second paragraph at from 130 to 140 words per minute; the third paragraph at from 170 to 180 words; and the fourth paragraph just as fast as the speaker can talk and make sense in his words. Here is the test copy:

Good evening, everyone. I'm making this test recording to hear what my voice sounds like when I'm talking at different rates of speed. Right now, I am speaking at about the same number of words I'd use in everyday conversation. Does my voice sound natural? Do I sound conversational? Maybe I'm speaking a little faster than I do when carrying on a conversation with a friend. What do you think? Sometimes when reading from prepared material, as I am doing right now, one has a tendency to speak faster than when he is making up his words as he goes along.

Well, listen to my voice while I'm speaking at the rate of between 130 and 140 words a minute. This is the average rate of speed used by President Roosevelt when he speaks and he is considered to have one of the finest radio deliveries of any speaker on the air. Do I seem to be speaking slower or faster? Does the change in speed give my voice better tone quality or isn't there much difference? Speaking at this rate of speed makes for better enunciation, flexibility in voice, better tone quality, and easier listening, according to those who think they know something about radio speaking. Now I'm going to pause. (*Pause.*) Now I'll pause again. (*Pause.*) They say that in radio speaking, a correctly placed pause is "the pause that refreshes." It relieves the monotony of constant pacing. Well, how does it sound to you? Have I been reading this at too constant a pace? We shall see—we shall see—or maybe I should say, we shall hear after I've finished making this record.

Now I'm going to speed up. I'm going to speak at about 170 to 180 a minute. They tell me that this speed is the ideal rate for the average news announcer. What is it doing to the tonal quality of my voice? Is my voice lower or higher? It should be higher. Maybe my voice isn't as easy to listen to at this speed. Does the added speed seem to add any life to my voice? At this faster rate I am less likely to use that pause that refreshes than when speaking at the slower rate. However, I should employ the pause no matter how fast I speak. If I don't I'll sound monotonous and to sound monotonous is the worst sin a radio speaker can be guilty of. Am I guilty or innocent? Guilty as the devil, I'm afraid. Well, you haven't heard anything yet.

Get an earful of this. I'm going to speak just as fast as I can. I should be able to speak at a speed of 200 to 240 words per minute. How am I doing? How would you like to have me speak for half an hour at this rate of speed? You would? I was afraid of that. If I talked at this rate of speed for half an hour they'd probably have to place me in an oxygen tent, if I lasted that long. You ought to try this some time. It's not so easy as it sounds— or does it sound easy? Of course, I could speak faster but I'm trying to make sense in what I'm saying and yet speak as fast as I can without making a mistake in enunciation. Do I sound monotonous? Where's that pause that refreshes? Speed certainly does things to one's voice and anyone listening to this must be taking plenty of punishment. Well, this is just about enough of this and now, to demonstrate what happens to the voice when I reduce this speed to about 140 words per minute, I'm going to put on the brakes and go into low gear.

Now I'm speaking again at about 140 words per minute. Do you notice the difference? Is the tonal quality improved by this slower rate? Well, this test recording should teach me a whole lot about the pitch, tonal quality, and clearness in my speaking voice when speaking at different speeds. It should prove that the best radio speakers know their business when they talk at an average speed of between 130 and 140 words a minute. Well, thanks for listening. What's the verdict?

Prior to making this test record it will be well to do a rehearsal, reading with a stop watch handy. Time each paragraph as you read it. Make sure that you train your ear to recognize the different speeds so that you'll be able to read at the designated rates.

Yes, recordings properly employed will go a long way in helping you to criticize your own work. And don't forget to use them after you start broadcasting. Professionals do, and they have a reason for it. That reason should be clear to you now.

CHAPTER XVIII

Voice Chart and Exercises

You've got to have a good ear if you want a good voice. That goes for speaking as well as for singing. Most of us hear well enough but we don't pay conscious attention to sound. We don't discriminate accurately because we haven't trained our ears, through practice, to be alert and sensitive.

If you know the vocabulary of voice and the fundamental analysis of tone, you have a proper focus and a point of view to begin with. You will improve your own voice as soon as you can make a fairly accurate, detailed judgment about others. It isn't enough to say vaguely that a voice is pleasing or tiresome, or good or bad or fair. Can you give the reasons why the voice makes the favorable or unfavorable impression? Can you give specific advice on how to improve it, how to eliminate the sour notes your ear has distinguished?

College students of speech are required to make frequent appraisals of voices heard on the air. They often make their own charts based on the four elements of voice. Every sound has these four elements of *quality*, *force*, *time*, and *pitch*, whether it is made by an automobile horn, a cow's moo, a train whistle, or the human voice. Each element may be subdivided into many details, most of which have already been discussed in several chapters of this book. Quality, for instance, includes breathing, relaxation, reso-

215

nance, mood, emotion, and articulation. Pitch includes inflection, modulation of individual words and phrases, as well as changes in the characteristic voice level.

For your convenience in studying and testing voices we are listing the questions that should be asked and answered in order to get a definite and accurate "profile" or evaluation. Of course, your judgment on many things will be subjective, the result of personal taste. You may like what others dislike. Even well-known singers are not enjoyed by all listeners. As for speaking voices, they are affected by environment, and people like what they are used to. The New Englander may not dislike the accents and intonations of Southerners and Westerners, but he may think his own are standard or preferable.

Whether you are right or wrong about certain characteristics of voice is not important in your first ratings. What counts is that you are forcing yourself to be aware of many things that you overlooked and didn't hear in your casual listening. Reflecting on these matters and practicing with the exercises that you discover are needed will condition your voice to ready and flexible expression of your thought and mood. Here is the list.

QUALITY

Is the voice thin or flat?

Does it sound as if it didn't have enough breath support?

Has it the fullness of tone that depends on the deeper, diaphragmatic breathing?

Is the breathing rhythmic and controlled, or does the voice sound jerky, uneven, spasmodic, or hurried?

Is the voice relaxed?

Does it sound hard, husky, throaty, guttural, squeaky, or strained?

Do the words seem to be made easily at the lips or do they sound as though they were squeezed from the back of the throat?

Is the tone bright? warm? sincere?

Is it affected? pompous? personal or impersonal? dull? heavy? overdramatic?

Are there ring and resonance in the tone, a continuous line of rich, humming quality?

Is the diction, the enunciation, satisfactory? Is it clear or inaudible? mumbled or unaffectedly correct?

Is it cultivated, crude, or careless?

What words were slurred?

What words reveal bad speech habits?

Is the quality conversational?

Why is the nonconversational style of speakers like Walter Winchell, Gabriel Heatter, and Edwin C. Hill effective?

Does the speaker reflect the mood appropriate to his material?

FORCE

Is the voice vital and confident? overconfident?

Does it sound positive enough—experienced? or does it sound negative—inexperienced? Is it a voice of authority?

Is the force explosive, indignant, irritating, overdramatic?

Is it effusive, sepulchral, "ministerial," full of reverence and awe?

Is it expulsive—the normal type of vigorous force that you hear in spirited conversation?

Is the force monotonous? Are words stressed too regularly?

Is the force too loud, exaggerated, insincere?

TIME

Does the speaker have the broken rhythm of talk?

Does he sound as if he were ad-libbing, not reading?

Does he say *well* and *uh* once in a while to give the illusion of chat?

Is the rate of speaking fast, slow, or moderate?

Are there enough pauses? Are they skillfully spaced?

Is the rate monotonous?

Does the speaker sound hurried or nervous?

Does he dawdle or race?

Are there poise and variety in the speaker's timing?

Are the phrase units natural and spontaneous, or are they controlled too much by the punctuation?

Was the talk begun slowly, in comfortable, intimate style?

How many words a minute did the speaker average?

Was the rate too fast for good articulation?

PITCH

Is the pitch too low? too high?

Does the speaker change his pitch level often enough to indicate change in topic or mood?

Should he speak faster or slower to get a better pitch level?

Is the inflection—up and down strokes on words and phrases—adequate to give the full meaning?

Is the inflection monotonous?

Does it sound like reading instead of talking?

Is the inflection stimulating? overdone? animated? thoughtful?

You will think of other questions, but if you answer carefully those given above, you will make encouraging progress, especially if you practice often with some of the exercises given below. In fact, you have in these few pages a complete program for home study in voice training.

BREATHING

1. Give the diaphragm exercise. Pant vigorously: *Hah, hay, hee, high, ho, hoo.*

2. Sing out boldly with these:

    a. Charge, Chester, charge!

    b. On, Stanley, on!

    c. On your marks! Ready! Go!

3. Inhale.   Whistle as you exhale, holding a note as long as you can.   Keep the whistle steady, without quavering.   **Practice** until you can hold the sound 30 seconds.

4. Say each of these sentences on one breath:

> *a.* Thou wouldst not play false, and yet wouldst wrongly win.
>
> *b.* Rich gifts wax poor when givers prove unkind.
>
> *c.* I am the very model of a modern major-general,
>   I've information vegetable, animal, and mineral.

5. Read these four lines slowly and rhythmically, breathing as often as you like.

> Gold!   Gold!   Gold!   Gold!
> Bright and yellow, hard and cold,
> Molten, graven, hammered, and rolled;
> Heavy to get and light to hold.

RELAXATION

1. Give the lips plenty of exercise to make them flexible and relaxed.   Say:

> *a. wee-woo-wye-way; wee-woo-wye-way.*
>
> *b.* With which winsome little witch were you working?
>
> *c.* Ah!   Sweet is Tipperary in the springtime of the year!
>
> *d.* I must go down to the seas again, to the lonely sea and the sky,
>   And all I ask is a tall ship and a star to steer her by.

2. Exercise the jaw on the vowels.   Say:

> *a. Ah, ay, ee, eye, oh, you.*
>
> *b.* Round and round the rock the rugged rascal ran.
>
> *c. Yah-hoo, yah-hoo, yah-hoo.*
>
> *d. Mee-ow-oo, mee-ow-oo, mee-ow-oo.*
>
> *e.* Sunset and evening star,
>   And one clear call for me!

3. Keep the throat open and relaxed while you say:

    a. "Down, down, down to the bottom of the sea." Go down as far as you can without getting the last low note stuck in your throat.

    b. Send the voice up and out on this:

        Will ye give it up to slaves?
        Will ye look for greener graves?
        Hope ye mercy still?

    c. Imagine you have a megaphone for this one. If you give it with a hearty, buoyant, chanting quality, your voice is relaxed.

        Yo ho, lads! Yo ho, yo ho!
        The captain calls to all below!

RESONANCE

Practice the hum in *l, m, n,* and *ng.* Get the singing speaking voice. Chanting is good practice until you realize that ordinary talk, the conversational tone, should have the resonance of sympathy, cheerfulness, vigor. Go oratorical until you're not afraid of the bigger, bolder tone. Then try that mellow, richer quality on more subdued and casual passages. Try these, and don't let them sound like a weather report. It's the emotional quality that breaks through the dry crust of our bookkeeping tones.

1. Dr. Talmage has drawn for you, with a master's hand, the picture of your returning armies. He has told you how, in the pomp and circumstance of war, they came back to you, marching with proud and victorious tread, reading their glory in a nation's eyes! Will you bear with me while I tell you of another army that sought its home at the close of the late war—an army that marched home in defeat and not in victory—in pathos and not in splendor, but in glory that equaled yours, and to hearts as loving as ever welcomed heroes home! Let me picture to you the footsore Confederate soldier, as buttoning up in his faded gray jacket the parole which was to bear testimony to his children of his fidelity and faith, he turned his way southward from

Appomattox in April, 1865. Think of him as ragged, half-starved, heavy-hearted, enfeebled by want and wounds. Having fought to exhaustion, he surrenders his gun, wrings the hands of his comrades in silence, and lifting his tear-stained and pallid face for the last time to the graves that dot the old Virginia hills, pulls his gray cap over his brow and begins the slow and painful journey. What does he find—let me ask you who went to your homes eager to find, in the welcome you had justly earned, full payment for four years' sacrifice—what does he find when, having followed the battle-stained cross against overwhelming odds, dreading death not half so much as surrender, he reaches the home he left so prosperous and beautiful? He finds his house in ruins, his farm devastated, his slaves free, his stock killed, his barns empty, his trade destroyed, his money worthless, his social system, feudal in its magnificence, swept away; his people without law or legal status; his comrades slain, and the burdens of others heavy on his shoulders. Crushed by defeat, his very traditions are gone. Without money, credit, employment, material, or training; and beside all this, confronted with the gravest problem that ever met human intelligence—the establishing of a status for the vast body of his liberated slaves.

HENRY W. GRADY.

2. Roll on, thou deep and dark blue Ocean—roll!
    Ten thousand fleets sweep over thee in vain,
Man marks the earth with ruin—his control
    Stops with the shore;—upon the watery plain
    The wrecks are all thy deed, nor doth remain
A shadow of man's ravage, save his own,
    When for a moment like a drop of rain,
He sinks into thy depths with bubbling groan,
    Without a grave, unknelled, uncoffined, and unknown.

LORD BYRON.

3. He has done the murder. No eye has seen him; no ear has heard him. The secret is his own, and it is safe! Ah, gentlemen,

that was a dreadful mistake! Such a secret can be safe nowhere. The whole creation of God has neither nook nor corner where the guilty can bestow it and say it is safe. Not to speak of the eye which pierces through all disguises, and beholds everything as in the splendor of noon, such secrets of guilt are never safe from detection, even by men. True it is, generally speaking, that "murder will out." . . . A thousand eyes turn at once to explore every man, every thing, every circumstance connected with the time and place; a thousand ears catch every whisper; a thousand excited minds dwell intensely on the scene, shedding all their light, and ready to kindle the slightest circumstance into a blaze of discovery.

Daniel Webster.

4. I have traveled in the course of the month I have been on this side of the Atlantic some thousands of miles in Canada and in the United States of America, and my first, and I think my deepest, impression is the vastness of these two great countries of infinite resources and of endless possibilities. There was an old Welsh peasant who had lived inland all his life and had a very hard time of it on his small farm, who, in his old age, came for the first time to the seaside, and when he saw the sea he said, "Thank God for something of which there seems to be plenty."

David Lloyd George.

5. Today so many thousands of welcome telegrams and postcards and letters of birthday greetings have poured in on me in the White House that I want to take this opportunity of thanking all of you who have sent them. From the bottom of my heart I am grateful to you for your thought. I wish I could divide myself by six thousand and attend in person each and every one of these birthday parties. I cannot do that, but I can be and I am with you all in spirit and in the promotion of this great cause for which we all are crusading.

No man ever had a finer birthday remembrance from his friends and fellows than you have given me tonight. It is with a humble and thankful heart that I accept this tribute through

me to the stricken ones of our great national family. I thank
you, but lack the words to tell you how deeply I appreciate what
you have done, and I bid you good night on what to me is the
happiest birthday I ever have known.

FRANKLIN D. ROOSEVELT.

See Chap. XII for other exercises in breathing, relaxation, resonance, and mood.

FORCE

Remember that every passage is an exercise in all the
elements of voice. We select passages that display one or
another more obviously to focus on a student's special
problem. The timid, diffident speaker should practice
with selections that encourage him to speak up. He
needs more confidence, drive, force. Now this first passage
requires conversational ease and authority. Hamlet knows
a good deal about acting, and he is telling the actors how
he wants the lines of his play spoken. He gives sound
advice and at the same time reveals scorn of the "ham"
actors of his own day. This is also a fine exercise for neat
and "tripping" diction, and for timing that breaks up the
lines so that they sound like talk. Give it plenty of pauses.
Notice that there is a great variety of force. Don't pound
along on one note.

1. Speak the speech, I pray you, as I pronounced it to you,
trippingly on the tongue: but if you mouth it, as many of your
players do, I had as lief the town-crier spoke my lines. Nor do
not saw the air too much with your hand, thus; but use all gently:
for in the very torrent, tempest, and, as I may say, whirlwind of
your passion, you must acquire and beget a temperance that may
give it smoothness. O, it offends me to the soul to hear a robus-
tious periwig-pated fellow tear a passion to tatters, to very rags, to
split the ears of the groundlings, who, for the most part, are

capable of nothing but inexplicable dumb-shows and noise: I would have such a fellow whipped for o'erdoing Termagant; it out-Herods Herod: pray you, avoid it.

Be not too tame neither, but let your own discretion be your tutor: suit the action to the word, the word to the action. . . . O, there be players that I have seen play, and heard others praise, and that highly, not to speak it profanely, that neither having the accent of Christians, . . . pagan, nor man, have so strutted and bellowed, that I have thought some of nature's journeymen had made men, and not made them well, they imitated humanity so abominably.

SHAKESPEARE.

Lift up your voice with exulting power in this next passage.   Give it with a strong, chanting resonance.

2. Lift up your heads, O ye gates; and be ye lifted up, ye everlasting doors; and the King of glory shall come in.

Who is this King of glory?   The Lord strong and mighty, the Lord mighty in battle.

Lift up your heads, O ye gates; even lift them up, ye everlasting doors; and the King of glory shall come in.

Who is this King of glory?   The Lord of hosts, he is the King of glory.

PSALM XXIV.

The following requires a wide variety of pause and inflection as well as energetic force.   And it is a good test of articulation.

3.   On the Earl's cheek the flush of rage
                O'ercame the ashen hue of age:
            Fierce he broke forth:—"And darest thou, then,
                To beard the lion in his den,
                    The Douglas in his hall?
                And hopest thou hence unscathed to go?—

No, by Saint Bride of Bothwell, no!
Up drawbridge, grooms—what, warder, ho!
    Let the portcullis fall."

Sir Walter Scott, Marmion.

Here is something from an after-dinner speech—humorous, ironic. The speaker's facial expression and bearing no doubt helped a great deal to suggest the playful and yet subtle mood. Can you do it by voice alone? Give it an easy, intimate, round-table mood spiced with dry humor. Give it slowly enough with the pauses that make the comedy spontaneous.

4. I can't overlook this opportunity to proclaim that I have on my home one of the best and biggest mortgages in my town. That is to say, the biggest for the size of the property. I'd like to call attention, also, to its durability. Although that mortgage has been on my home for many years, exposed to all sorts of weather and changes of fortune, it's just as good and just as big today as it was the day I put it on. I have seen holes come and holes go in the roof of my house, but never the tiniest loophole in the mortgage.

For a long time my home has been the feeding ground of a large and enterprising colony of termites. It's a common thing to see an insolent family of termites, gorged on some of the choicest studding and foundation timbers in my house, who have tapered off their meal with choice sections of the dining-room floor and a big helping of doorjamb—I say, it's not unusual to see such a group of consumers lolling about, picking their teeth while digesting their meal, casting an appraising eye on the walnut staircase, but never taking the slightest interest in the mortgage.

Harvey T. Harrison.

TIME

Good timing is the test of the actor. He must make everything sound so natural, as if he were speaking his words for the first time, that it seems easy. Yet this imitation of life is successful chiefly because the actor hears the rhythms of the talk appropriate to the situation. He knows that all talk is full of pauses of different length, that the rate of speaking may change considerably in the course of a few lines, and that no rate should be kept up uniformly. Variety is absolutely necessary to hold attention. The actor wants short sentences and not many at a time. He often requests a playwright to recast a passage that sounds literary and not the actual talk of the characters. His sensitive ear warns him that the stuff is dead because it has a false rhythm—the timing is wrong and can't be convincingly corrected by the actor.

These two passages from Dicken's *A Christmas Carol* give you interesting variety in the timing of informal speech.

1. Marley was dead, to begin with. There is no doubt whatever about that. The register of his burial was signed by the clergyman, the clerk, the undertaker, and the chief mourner. Scrooge signed it. And Scrooge's name was good upon 'Change for anything he chose to put his hand to.

Old Marley was as dead as a door-nail.

2. Oh! but he was a tight-fisted hand at the grindstone, Scrooge! a squeezing, wrenching, grasping, scraping, clutching, covetous old sinner! Hard and sharp as flint, from which no steel had ever struck out generous fire; secret, and self-contained, and solitary as an oyster. The cold within him froze his old features, nipped his pointed nose, shriveled his cheek, stiffened his gait; made his eyes red, his thin lips blue; and spoke out shrewdly in his grating voice.

CHARLES DICKENS.

Here is a good combination of force and time. The passion, the eloquence, must be controlled. The pauses must be impressive, the upstrokes and downstrokes of inflection sweeping and incisive.

3. There is no retreat but in submission and slavery! Our chains are forged. Their clanking may be heard on the plains of Boston! The war is inevitable—and let it come!—I repeat, sir, let it come! It is vain, sir, to extenuate the matter. Gentlemen may cry, peace, peace!—but there is no peace. The war has actually begun!

The next gale that sweeps from the north will bring to our ears the clash of resounding arms! Our brethren are already in the field! Why stand we here idle? What is it that gentlemen wish? What would they have? Is life so dear, or peace so sweet, as to be purchased at the price of chains and slavery? Forbid it, Almighty God! I know not what course others may take; but, as for me, give me liberty or give me death!

PATRICK HENRY.

Here is something that should make the diaphragm work through emotional stimulus—the cunning gusto of a madman describing his crime. He speaks with relish and fervor, but he speaks slowly enough so that you won't miss any of the details he wishes you to appreciate.

4. It is impossible to say how first the idea entered my brain; but once conceived, it haunted me day and night. Object there was none. Passion there was none. I loved the old man. He had never wronged me. He had never given me insult. For his gold I had no desire. I think it was his eye! yes, it was this! He had the eye of a vulture—a pale blue eye, with a film over it. Whenever it fell upon me, my blood ran cold; and so by degrees—very gradually—I made up my mind to take the life of the old man, and thus rid myself of the eye forever.

Now this is the point. You fancy me mad. Madmen know nothing. But you should have seen *me*. You should have seen how wisely I proceeded—with what caution—with what foresight—with what dissimulation I went to work! I was never kinder to the old man than during the whole week before I killed him. And every night, about midnight, I turned the latch of his door and opened it so gently! And then, when I had made an opening sufficient for my head, I put in a dark lantern, all closed, closed, so that no light shone out, and then I thrust in my head. Oh, you would have laughed to see how cunningly I thrust it in! I moved slowly—very, very slowly, so that I might not disturb the old man's sleep. It took me an hour to place my whole head in the opening so far that I could see him as he lay upon his bed. Ha—would a madman have been so wise as this? And then, when my head was well in the room, I undid the lantern cautiously—oh, so cautiously—cautiously (for the hinges creaked)—I undid it just so much that a single thin ray fell upon the vulture eye. And this I did for seven long nights— every night just at midnight—but I found the eye always closed; and so it was impossible to do the work; for it was not the old man who vexed me, but his Evil Eye.

EDGAR ALLAN POE, *The Tell-tale Heart.*

PITCH

The first problem is to find your natural pitch level. People often speak on a higher or lower level because of self-consciousness or embarrassment.

High pitch usually accompanies a rapid, nervous rate of speaking. The speaker should practice relaxing the whole body as well the mind and the throat. He should speak much slower, and aim the tone at the hard palate or lips.

Too low a pitch may be the result of an impassive, phlegmatic disposition that lacks interest in people or things. It doesn't make sufficient response to the stimuli around it. Stimuli should stimulate.

Sometimes an unresponsive voice lacks flexibility simply because the speaker has assumed a certain manner and attitude toward others—a kind of defense mechanism—

and his voice makes a routine grunt in reply to anything that is said to him.

Business executives often have a monotone—heavy, abrupt, or affectedly bright—in which they regularly address subordinates. A man may say "Good morning!" in such a harsh tone that it sounds like "Go to the devil." He means all right, but he has only one tune, learned in office practice, and he gives out with it, through habit, in every speech situation. A voice recording would give him a shock, and he needs it to break through this crust of crusty habit.

Then there is the introvert who has a shy and retiring temperament. His voice is flat, monotonous, subdued. He needs to "mix" with people and learn to like them.

All persons with a chronic, expressionless low pitch should practice with exercises that demand daring and lift, and a variety of gay, buoyant tones. Once they have the feel of these they will not return to that drab, anemic quality.

Sprightly dialogue is especially helpful. Contrasting characters and imitating different voices, even if it isn't done very well, give a sense of drama and excitement that makes for flexibility. Try these passages, and don't be afraid to exaggerate.

TO RAISE LOW PITCH

1. BOB: Are you going to get that collar button or do I have to go down there and get married in front of two hundred people with my collar ends waving in the breeze like a sailboat?

ARCHIE: Sh-h! Sh-h! Sure, I will—only don't get jumpy, Bob. (*He starts for the door.*) Oh, say, by the way—do you want me to stand close—or farther away?

BOB: When? Where?

ARCHIE: At the altar. You know some grooms like to look independent—and some like to be sort of buoyed up.

BOB: Oh, I don't care. Just give me plenty of room to swing my arms—and don't trip me.

ARCHIE: I know. That's the way I had to do with Dick Mayfield. Only he started off on the wrong foot. (*Coming back.*) Bob, let me caution you—whatever you do, don't start off on the wrong foot. Otherwise, you know, we'll come in skipping and jumping and catching up—I'll be embarrassed to death.

BOB: *You'll* be embarrassed?

ARCHIE: Oh, well, you know everybody expects the groom to look like a fool, anyway. You're sure you know now which foot to start on?

BOB: Of course I do. (*Sticking out left foot.*) The right one.

ARCHIE: That's not your right foot.

BOB: All right then—we'll start on the left one.

ARCHIE: But we don't—we start on the right.

BOB: *All right! All right! Both feet!* I'll do a broad jump—only *are you going to get me a collar button?*

ARCHIE: Sure, I'm going. Only keep calm.

BOB: *I am calm!*[1]

JOHN KIRKPATRICK, *A Wedding.*

2. Old Fezziwig laid down his pen, and looked up at the clock, which pointed to the hour of seven. He rubbed his hands; adjusted his capacious waistcoat; laughed all over himself, from his shoes to his organ of benevolence; and called out, in a comfortable, oily, rich, fat, jovial voice—

"Yo ho, there! Ebenezer! Dick!"

Scrooge's former self, now grown a young man, came briskly in, accompanied by his fellow-'prentice.

"Dick Wilkins, to be sure!" said Scrooge to the Ghost. "Bless me, yes. There he is. He was very much attached to me, was Dick. Poor Dick! Dear, dear!"

"Yo ho, my boys!" said Fezziwig. "No more work tonight. Christmas Eve, Dick. Christmas, Ebenezer! Let's have the shutters up," cried old Fezziwig, with a sharp clap of his hands, "before a man can say Jack Robinson!"

You wouldn't believe how those two fellows went at it! They charged into the street with the shutters—one, two, three—had 'em up in their places—four, five, six—barred 'em and pinned 'em—seven, eight, nine—and came back before you could have got to twelve, panting like racehorses.

"Hilli-ho!" cried old Fezziwig, skipping down from the high desk with wonderful agility. "Clear away, my lads, and let's have lots of room here!"

CHARLES DICKENS.

To lower the pitch level, practice on dark, somber, melancholy passages. Prolong the vowels, speak slowly, and project the tone with good resonance.

TO LOWER THE PITCH

1. MACBETH: Wherefore was that cry?
   SEYTON: The queen, my lord, is dead.
   MACBETH: She should have died hereafter;
  There would have been a time for such a word.
  To-morrow, and to-morrow, and to-morrow,
  Creeps in this petty pace from day to day,
  To the last syllable of recorded time;
  And all our yesterdays have lighted fools
  The way to dusty death.   Out, out, brief candle!
  Life's but a walking shadow, a poor player
  That struts and frets his hour upon the stage
  And then is heard no more; it is a tale
  Told by an idiot, full of sound and fury,
  Signifying nothing.

SHAKESPEARE.

2. Lead out the pageant: sad and slow,
  As fits an universal woe;
  Let the long, long procession go,
  And let the sorrowing crowd about it grow,
  And let the mournful, martial music blow;
  The last great Englishman is low.

LORD ALFRED TENNYSON.

3. "Everything comes to light, Nancy, sooner or later. When God Almighty wills it, our secrets are found out. I've lived with a great secret on my mind, but I'll keep it from you no longer. I wouldn't have you know it by somebody else, and not by me— I wouldn't have you find it out after I'm dead. I'll tell you now. It's been 'I will' and 'I won't' with me all my life—I'll make sure of myself now."

Nancy's utmost dread had returned. The eyes of the husband and wife met with awe in them, as at a crisis which suspended affection.

"Nancy," said Godfrey slowly, "when I married you, I hid something from you—something I ought to have told you. That woman Marner found dead in the snow—Eppie's mother—that wretched woman—was my wife; Eppie is my child."

GEORGE ELIOT, *Silas Marner.*

INFLECTION

Inflection is derived from a Latin word meaning *to bend.* It is the bends that are seriously missing in the average script reading. As Woolbert and Smith say in *The Fundamentals of Speech,* "Every syllable involves a slide upward or downward." Sometimes, indeed, a syllable has both slides as in "Well, whát abóut ìt?"

Most syllables have the upward slide because they do not indicate finality, or the end of the thought. They suggest incompleteness or suspension of the thought.

The downward slide is much less common. It usually indicates the end of the sentence, or something of weight, assurance, or deep feeling.

It isn't necessary to study rules in regard to inflection because they tell you only what you already know. They are simply the observations made after listening to lively conversation. Almost everybody inflects well in pleasant, intimate, unrestrained talk. The exceptions are those

persons who are affected and "put on" insincere inflections
—you recognize them at once—and those who are inhibited
by bad habits of speech or by a lack of ease and poise.

We inflect according to the meaning we wish to put into
words. We do this accurately and fully in private talk,
but the moment we read a script—even one we have
written ourselves—we are likely to speak words instead of
ideas. Now the words are only black marks on white
paper, and their surface or obvious content is only part
of the complete meaning. If we get too literal with them
and forget that they are only symbols of thought and feeling
which must be made revealing to the reader by our personal
intent, we fail to give the free and varied inflection of talk.

Take the single word *yes*, for instance. By itself, and
even in the context of a phrase, it may have little meaning.
On the other hand, the way you utter it may give it a world
of meaning. In fact, you can say it to give a great variety
of meanings.

Just to be sure that you appreciate the importance of this
obvious matter, inflect *yes* correctly for each of the following
meanings:

1. Yes. (I will go.) A promise.
2. Yes? (Is that so?) Mild interest.
3. Yes. (He died today.) Sorrow.
4. Yes. (It *is* a fine morning.) Cheerfulness.
5. Yes. (I will marry you.) Tenderness.
6. Yes. (That's true, but you overlook something.) Agreeing with reservations.
7. Yes! (We win.) Exultation.
8. Yes. (We lose.) Dejection.
9. Yes. (This is Jones speaking.) Over the telephone.
10. Yes. (I suppose so.) Doubtfully.
11. Yes. (You will go!) Angrily.

12. Yes.   (Go on!   Go on!)   Excitedly, in suspense.
13. Yes.   (Oh yeah!)   Jeeringly.
14. Yes!   (Of course!   How many times must I tell you?)
Impatiently.
15. Yes.   (What of it?)   Defiantly.
16. Yes?   (Yes?   He said yes?)   Surprise and incredulity.
17. Yes.   (He will—not.)   Sarcasm.
18. Yes.   (Uh-huh.)   Absent-mindedly.
19. Yes.   (We all have our troubles.)   Resignation.
20. Yes!   (You bet I will!)   Hearty assent.
21. Yes.   (I am guilty.)   Reluctant confession.
22. Yes!   (Hurry, for God's sake!)   Agonized fright.

You have already had considerable practice in inflection
if you have done the other exercises in this list. Let go
now with plenty of bends on these last three, and prove
that you have mastered conversational timing, confident,
authoritative attack (not too loud), and varied, meaningful
inflection.

1. A director of an amateur production could do nothing with
a rather diffident young fellow who was supposed to be shot, not
very seriously. He was to cry out with plenty of animation and
excitement, "I'm shot!" but in spite of all coaching, the cry was
an indifferent, perfunctory grunt. On the night of the play
the director, without telling the player, put catchup into the gun,
so that there might be a realistic display of blood on the victim.
At the sound of the gun the boy staggered a little, as he had
rehearsed, and said in his usual languid manner, "I'm shot."
Just then he looked down at his vest, saw what he thought was
blood, and yelled, "My God!   I *am* shot!"

2. And so the undergraduate stretches his legs before the hearth
and hears the wisdom of the "Old Grad." In his day, it seems,
things were different. The students were not such mollycoddles,
the beer flowed more freely, and the faculty did not try to run
things. . . . "I tell you, boys," cries the Old Grad, warming

his feet by the fire and his imagination by the wonder of the freshmen, "it is not what you learn in your classes that counts. Books, lectures, recitations—you will forget all that. Nobody cares after you graduate whether you know any Latin or algebra, unless you are a teacher, and no man can afford to be a teacher nowadays. But you will remember the college life as long as you live."

Some of the alumni would have a different story to tell, no doubt, but they do not get back often for fraternity initiations. Perhaps they are too busy.

Whatever we may think of the "Old Grad's" remarks, the idea does prevail in many a college that the most important enterprises are found in the side shows, conducted by the students themselves, while the faculty present more or less buncombe performances in the main tent.

WILLIAM TRUFANT FOSTER.

3. We are up to the neck in the class war. What is it that is wrong with our present way of doing things? It is not that we cannot produce enough goods. Our machines turn out enough work in an hour as ten thousand hand workers used to; but it is not enough for a country to produce goods, it must distribute them as well. And this is where our system breaks down hopelessly. Everybody ought to be living quite comfortably by working four or five hours a day with two Sundays in the week, yet millions of laborers die in the workhouse or on the dole after sixty years of hard toil so that a few babies may have hundreds of thousands of dollars before they are born.

As I see it, this is not to be argued about but to take sides about. It is stupid and wicked on the face of it, and it will smash us and our civilization if we do not absolutely reform it. Yet we do nothing but keep up a perpetual ballyhoo about bolshevism, fascism, communism, liberty, dictators, democracy, and all the rest of it.

The very first lesson of the new history dug up for us by Professor Flinders Petrie during my lifetime is that no civilization, however splendid, illustrious, and like our own, can stand up against the social resentments and class conflicts which follow a silly misdistribution of wealth, labor, and leisure; and it is the one history lesson that is never taught in our schools, thus condemning the saying of the German philosopher Hegel, "We learn from history that we never learn anything from history." Think it over. So long; so long!

GEORGE BERNARD SHAW, NBC, November 2, 1937.

A GLOSSARY OF RADIO TERMS
FOR SPEAKERS

across-mike. Projection of the voice almost parallel with the face of the microphone.

ad-lib. Extemporization of lines not written in the script.

adenoid. A voice that is "tight."

audition. A microphone test under actual broadcasting conditions.

balance. A voice level of the speaker's tonal range.

beam. Usually referred to as "on the beam." A direct line from the face of the microphone.

bending the needle. Projecting an unexpected volume of sound into the microphone so that the needle on the volume indicator violently hits the top of the scale.

blasting. Too much volume, resulting in voice distortion.

board. The engineer's control panel.

bring it up. Increase the voice volume.

commercial. A sponsored program.

commercial credits. Sponsored announcements.

corny. Unsophisticated, stale.

control room. Housing for the monitoring equipment.

cue. The closing words of an actor's speech; a signal to start.

cue sheet. An orderly tabulation of program routine containing all cues.

cushion. A portion of a speech added to lengthen the talk if desired.

dead microphone. A microphone not connected or out of order.

down in the mud. Low in volume or clarity.

fade. A decrease of volume.

fade-out. A complete decrease of volume to zero.

free lance.　Personnel not employed regularly by the station.

gain.　Control of volume used in transmission.

kill.　To omit portions of the speech entirely.

live studio.　One that is acoustically reverberant.

mike mugger.　A speaker who insists on working too close to the microphone.

mix.　To combine the input of two or more microphones to effect a complete balance.

mixing.　Blending sound.

nemo.　Any program originating outside the studio.

off mike.　A speaker's position away from the microphone.

on the button.　Ending exactly on time.　Same as "on the nose."

out in the alley.　Out of microphone range.

peak.　The maximum point of the needle swing on the volume indicator.

playback.　The playing of a recording for audition purposes.

stretch it out.　To slow up the reading so that program will finish on time.

time check.　Synchronization of timepieces with the studio clock.

v. i.　Volume indicator.

velocity.　A ribbon-type microphone.

INDEX

239

Date Due

OCT 1 1 '48			
2-4-49			
FEB 2 1 '50			
FEB 1 1 '52			
Mar 25 52			
APR 7 53			
OCT 6 '55			
FEB 2 0 '56			
MAR 8 '56			
DEC 2 0 '56			
DEC 2 0 '56			
JAN 1 7 '57			
FEB 1 9 '57			
OCT 1 0 58			
OCT 1 8 59			
JAN 2 9 59			
FEB 1 3 '59			
JUL 1 6 '59			
MAY 2 6 '60			
JAN 1 8 1982 FEB 1 8 1982			
FEB 0 3 1991			